THE
ARENA
by Calvin Schiraldi

The true story about one man's search for excellence
and the price he paid for daring to achieve it.

ISBN: 978-1-7378012-0-7

Book Cover by RSD Design

Book Interior by
Anita Stumbo, DFW Signature Press

This book is dedicated to my wife, Debbie, whose love and dedication gave me my life back.

ACKNOWLEDGMENTS

I WOULD LIKE TO THANK the following people who took the time to read the manuscript and provided me with invaluable feedback: Lance Winn, Tracey Thompson, Russell Sterns, Max Duncan, Patrice Scheier, Trey Boucvalt, Mackie Smith, Kenny K, Duncan Butler, Kevin Brown, Elizabeth Bartell, Mark Eckert, and Mike and Betti Tiner.

A special thanks to John Vondrak, who shared his immense editing talents for this project.

Finally, I'd like to thank David Koch. David and I have known each other for years, and he knows my story better than almost anyone. He was instrumental in organizing this project, and it would not have happened without him. Furthermore, I'm very grateful for the vision he had concerning my story, not to mention the appreciation he had for my journey. A heartfelt thanks, my man.

TABLE OF CONTENTS

PREFACE

ABOUT A YEAR AGO, I was traveling to South Texas with a friend on a hunting trip. As we drove, we passed the time talking about a variety of things. During our conversation, I shared with him an email that I had recently received from an anonymous sender. The message was raw and aggressive, but the most interesting thing about it was the fact that it focused on an event which had occurred more than three decades earlier. Deep down, it really bothered me, but I laughed it off as if it were no big deal. In truth, my outward response was just a protection mechanism I had mastered long ago. Perplexed by the whole scene and not believing it could be possible, my friend asked if he could read the actual text of the email. What he didn't know was that I had been receiving this nasty stuff in the form of phone calls, letters, and more, dating all the way back to 1986. Granted, they have since died down to almost nothing, but I still get them thirty-five years later. Completely dumbfounded by the contents of this email, my friend's reaction was immediate and very defensive of me, as if he could sense that this bothered me much more than I was letting on. "Screw that coward," he said. "What the hell are you doing reading anything from a piece of shit like that?" That was only a small part of his unfiltered reaction. He then blasted me for saving the email, went on a tirade about the perception of winners and losers, and ended with something that truly resonated. From his cell phone, he read to me Teddy Roosevelt's speech *The Man in the Arena,* which, believe it or not, I had never heard before.

I vividly recall those words, as they flowed through my mind like a breath of fresh air. I'm not overstating the moment when I say that this quote, from over a hundred years ago, was therapeutic. It touched me so deeply that it was like finding a panacea for a disease that I had written off as incurable long ago. Not only was it powerful and relevant, it lifted a crushing weight off of my shoulders—one I had struggled to carry for decades. In some ways, Roosevelt's words returned the dignity which had been taken, uncontested, so many years before. It also defended me in the most profound way imaginable, but most importantly, it had opened my eyes to just how deeply I had allowed a shadowy group of people to impact my life. If this sounds odd or over the top, it shouldn't. The truth is, I had been struggling with certain aspects of my life for a long time, and sometimes, when you're in a dark place, something just clicks and helps you escape. This quote did that for me.

As the weeks passed, my thoughts returned to *The Man in the Arena.* I found myself looking over my life's work and came to the sobering realization that there is a significant gap in how society perceives those who dare to enter the Arena. There is no middle ground—only winners and losers. Before I go any further, let me make something clear. I don't buy into the "everyone's a winner" bullshit, and I find the *trophies for all* mindset to be equally as appalling because it limits true development, discourages hard work, and stymies grit. My problem lies with the absolutes: winners and losers with no consideration, appreciation, or respect for the individual who earnestly entered the Arena prepared—with a fully conditioned mind and body—for victory, only to come up short. Again, don't get me wrong; winners deserve all the accolades, awards, and attention they receive. With hard work and talent, they came out on top in a competitive setting and reaped the rewards of that accomplishment—that's what it is all about. It's what we strive for and what makes competition so beautiful.

What I take exception to is the disdain, mocking, and total disregard shown toward those on the losing side of the contest—the ones who entered the Arena and gave everything they had, only in the end to be called weak, intimidated, or scared. More often than not, the labels don't come from fellow competitors (who know better) but from those who have never been in the Arena. These people know no boundaries and they base their comments on distant observation, which hinders their understanding of the complicated and dynamic nature of the situation they comment on. I understand that we're supposed to just ignore them, but by leaving them unchecked, they become emboldened, which in turn, allows them to set a narrative with no regard for truth, and more importantly, no understanding of the Arena. The picture they paint and the words they so callously throw around can follow a person for the rest of his life. There is something fundamentally wrong with this, and for the first time in my life, I finally realized it.

It also got me thinking. Do I really have to accept the possibility that my narrative has largely been written by people who don't even know me or my journey, who define me by one single pitch and worse, haven't the slightest clue of what it is like to be in the Arena? I could no longer accept that as a possibility.

It took years of battling demons—both real and perceived—before I finally had the confidence and clarity of mind to write this book. What's more, I'm an extremely private person, so publicly discussing my life was not something I was interested in doing. However, after reflecting on every aspect of the previous thirty-five years, I made the decision to enter the Arena one last time by writing a book that describes my journey and what it was like to live through it. Rest assured, this book does not serve as an excuse-ridden pity party written by a guy who didn't get it done in 1986. Far from it. I wrote this because, for better or worse, my life was forged in the Arena and I want to share that difficult, yet wonderful, experience with you.

The Arena is a unique and complicated place. Few understand it, and most who do, avoid it at all costs. It can be a place of great triumph and exhilarating, life-changing moments. Or, it can be a place of devastating beatdowns and unyielding pain. The meek are willfully oblivious to its existence and therefore know nothing of the riches it offers. Although widely understood as being tied exclusively to sports, the Arena can be any competitive environment that pits like-minded people against each other, with victory as the ultimate objective.

In addition to sports, the setting could be corporate, academic, artistic, or some other venue. It doesn't really matter. What matters is having the courage to do it and cultivating the desire and skills needed to come out on top. It requires a commitment to training both mind and body so that you give yourself the best possible chance to succeed. Most importantly, when the inevitable setback besieges you, it's about having the strength and courage to get back in and do it again, fully understanding the pain that potentially awaits you upon your return. This is the moment where you find yourself and where true, meaningful growth takes place. This is the Arena.

I spent a lifetime in this setting—and trust me—I have the battle scars to prove it. I've seen and felt things that most people never will. I have left that place a winner, and I've left it so badly beaten that I didn't know who I was anymore. With that said, there was one thing that didn't happen—I never quit. Throughout the following pages, I'll share my story with you, and hopefully you'll gain a newfound appreciation for the Arena and the countless brave souls (perhaps including yourself) who dare to enter it.

There's a special place in this world for those who risk it all to be great, and I can guarantee it is light years away from the delicate sideline dwellers who scour the perimeter of competition in search of the fallen. Don't misunderstand me, they too could benefit from this book, but it wasn't written *for* them. It was written for anyone who strives for excellence, knowing full well that if they wish to achieve it, they must enter a daunting and sometimes unforgiving place called the Arena.

My name is Calvin Schiraldi and this is my story.

Chapter 1

THE INTANGIBLE GIFT

Every person who wins in any undertaking must be willing to cut off all sources of retreat. Only by doing so can one be sure of maintaining the state of mind known as the 'burning desire to win'—essential to success. —NAPOLEON HILL

I KNOW FIRSTHAND what the Arena experience is like and have always had the utmost respect for it and what it meant to enter its gates. But I never feared it. You see, from the time I was a young boy, no matter what I was doing, I was determined to succeed. Whatever Arena I entered, I didn't play for fun—*I played to win.*

As I grew older and looked back at the achievements of my younger years, I found myself trying to identify precisely what had enabled me to accomplish those things. Was it natural abilities, where I went to school, or the coaches and teammates I was blessed to have along the way? I understood that each played an important role, but with me, the one thing above all others that gave me the edge in the Arena may not be what you think. I knew I possessed something, although I didn't quite understand what it was or from where it came. It was *an intangible gift,* with a presence that was always felt. Years later, it would come into greater focus, and I would understand what it was, how I got it, and the profound impact it would have on my career. Allow me to explain.

Most people realize that there are multiple factors as to why some athletes consistently succeed in the Arena. Traditionally, the two most mentioned also seem to be the most obvious—natural talent and good coaching. There's no denying the critical role that each plays. Obviously, natural talent is important. Bigger, faster, stronger isn't just a sports slogan; it plays a vital role in any competitive event. Look at Tiger Woods, Steffi Graf, Ted Williams, and Michael Jordan, to name a few. These athletes entered Arenas loaded with naturally gifted opponents, but more often than not, these superstars possessed a physical edge over their competitors. Woods brought to the tour a combination of strength and finesse the golf world had never seen before. Graf combined power with world-class foot speed and dominated women's tennis. Williams reportedly had 20/10 vision (which certainly didn't hurt when facing fastballs), and Jordan stood 6′6″ with hand-eye coordination that was off the charts. Their physical advantages are undeniable, so it's easy to tie these athletes' natural talents to their iconic careers. In fact, it's too easy. Defining the greatness of sports legends in such a way would not only be ignorant, it would be dismissive of what lies deeper inside them. You see, the sports world is littered with athletes who never won a thing, despite being gifted with incredible natural talent. Clearly, there must be more to winning than that.

Coaching is another factor. A coach who can inspire and make an athlete better plays a vital role in the art of winning. All accomplished people can trace their achievements back to those who helped them along the way. It may be a Little League coach, a high school counselor, or someone who trained them in college. Whomever or whenever, there was someone instrumental in their success. We're all familiar with great coaches like Tony La Russa, Pat Summitt, Vince Lombardi, and Pat Riley. Over the years, they have captured headlines for their winning ways as well as their mastery at teaching their respective sports to players. With that said, a great coach doesn't have to be a Hall of Famer. In fact, most successful athletes were never coached by legends. As I mentioned, influential coaches could be your parents, a high school coach, or someone as far back as Little League. It doesn't matter who they are. What matters is that someone had a significant, positive influence throughout the journey of a successful athlete's life, and without doubt, all played an important role in their success. But like talent, coaching alone will not get it done. The sports world is also littered with athletes who experienced phenomenal coaching and yet never won a thing. So what's missing?

The one factor most often overlooked is the "burning desire to win," which resides deep inside the heart of a successful athlete. In the discussion of consistent winning, this desire is underrated, misunderstood, and rarely finds its proper place alongside talent and coaching. It's underrated because it can be a driving force in how an athlete performs but is seldom given its due. It's misunderstood because it's constantly linked to things it is not. For example, you often hear people talk about hating to lose. They'll go to great lengths to explain to anyone who will listen just how competitive they are and how much losing bothers them. It's almost nauseating. Well, I have a newsflash: everyone hates to lose. However, hating to lose is not the same as the *burning desire to win.* How many times have we seen kids crying after losing a peewee football game, only to be playing and laughing twenty minutes later at a pizza place? Those tears were real, and they truly didn't want to lose, but that doesn't mean they had the *burning desire to win.* This concept is much deeper and more complex than that. For the record, I'm not picking on my little buddies in peewee football or singling out high school, college, or even professional athletes who may act in the same way. I am simply pointing out that hating to lose and the *burning desire to win* are not the same thing—not even close.

So what exactly is it? First and foremost, this desire comes from deep inside an athletes' soul. It's the driving force that allows them to dig deeper and see things that those who don't possess it never will. Sure, it makes losing very painful, but more importantly, it provides athletes with the motivation and strength to work harder outside the Arena in order to help mitigate the possibility of losing the next time they compete. This means extra time in the gym, early morning workouts, staying late after practice when everyone else has gone home, and studying the causes of their defeats in ways that most would not think to do so. Most importantly, when an athlete with this desire enters the Arena, winning is the only acceptable outcome. It's an extremely powerful force and can be the deciding factor on who gets to the winner's circle. It's not a guarantee, but it can be a definite edge. This is the *burning desire to win,* and it is one of the most overlooked, underrated, and underappreciated factors in understanding what makes people successful.

The next two questions are obvious: Where does it come from and, how do I get it? Those are million-dollar questions to which no one has the answer. Because the *burning desire to win* comes from deep inside, there's no magic formula or installation manual. Sometimes it's triggered by something simple, sometimes it develops from years of competing, and unfortunately, sometimes it never comes at all. That's just the way it is. As for me, I was one of the fortunate ones who had this desire from the time I was a young boy. I also know exactly where it came from.

I grew up in Austin, Texas, in a normal family with my parents and a younger sister. My mother was warm, gifted, and doted over her two children. She was the glue that kept the family together. My father was a great athlete and the star player for the 1952 Baytown, Texas, football team that made it to the state finals. He then went to Texas A&M University on a track scholarship. He was stern, to the point, and unlike my mother, there was very little that was warm about him. He would also become THE factor in instilling the *burning desire to win* deep within my soul. However, I probably wouldn't recommend using my example as a template.

Like many young boys, I worshipped my father. I found myself constantly looking for excuses to be around him and ways to get his approval. He was a good father, but not the type who would sit you on his lap and ask you how your day went. In fact, I don't ever remember a time where he gave me a hug. That's just not who he was.

Being that he was such a gifted athlete, my dad was really good at ping-pong and pool. Almost every weekend, Dad would take me to a downtown bar called Harold's, where we'd watch sports and shoot pool. Granted, this wasn't very traditional, and some might argue quite bizarre, but I saw it as an opportunity to be with my hero. At home, we would spend time together playing endless games of ping-pong. At first, this was all fun. After all, I was spending time with my dad, and to me, it didn't matter what we were doing.

But soon, that would change, and because of it, I would change. You see, when we were playing these games, there was no "Hey, son, this is how you hold the paddle," or "Here's the angle you'll need for this pool shot." No, these games were unapologetic ass whippings with a little mocking served up for dessert. To say he offered no mercy would be an understatement. Every day it was the same thing, and every day I'd come back for more. Occasionally, I would hit a good shot and found myself longing for a compliment, but none ever came. He would just finish the game by a lopsided margin and then go on to something else. After a while, I came to realize that he had no respect for my skills and to be honest, I felt he had no respect for me.

Keep in mind, I was just a kid at the time, so that feeling had a crushing effect on my spirit. Despite my never-ending efforts to do something that deserved this recognition, I simply couldn't get my father to recognize any positives in anything I did. Over time, this would have a profound effect on me, and I began to change. I became more hardened and felt a burning need to earn his respect. I also understood that the only way to accomplish that would be to win. In other words, to relieve my pain, I had to beat him at the games he had mastered for years. These were the same games, mind you, which I had only recently learned how to play. I could quit and stay away from him, which would have been easy to do, and to be honest, he wouldn't have given a shit. My other option was to find a way up that mountain without any help afforded by him. Thankfully, I chose not to quit. I remember going out to our garage and folding up half of the ping-pong table against the wall so I could practice by myself. This became my daily routine, and countless hours were spent this way.

While doing so, I dreamed about the respect I would receive from my father when the day of reckoning finally arrived. One night after work, I talked him into a ping-pong match, and it happened—I beat my father. I can't properly describe how exhilarating that moment was. My heart pounded, and I smiled from ear to ear, knowing the best was yet to come. That would be the acknowledgment, the "Attaboy!" or "Damn, you played a good game." But those words never came. My father quietly put his paddle down on the table and left the room. What's worse, we never played another game of ping-pong again.

I was devastated. Wasn't he aware of how hard I had worked or what this moment had meant to me? Was he not the least bit proud of how far I had come in a game that I had only recently learned to play? This was difficult as hell to swallow, and I resented him for this. At the time, I even thought I hated him. But Dad would never change. We would still shoot pool, and occasionally, I would beat him, always followed by the same result—no compliment or even an acknowledgment. He didn't stop playing me in pool because he knew I would never be able to consistently beat him, and he was right about that. Regardless, I never stopped trying and would spend the rest of my boyhood years in my quest to beat him. In reality, it was never about beating him; it was about a young boy yearning for his father's attention, his father's approval, and his father's respect. These feelings were deep-rooted and very real, and so was the desire to do anything to earn what my father was denying me.

Looking back, I can't adequately express how these experiences forged me. Throughout my entire sports career, I was in search of, and even craving, my father's approval. I wanted respect from the most important male figure in my life, and no matter how great the victory, this respect was what I desired most. This affirmation, recognition, compliment, or whatever you want to call it was that important, and yet, as a young boy, I would never experience it. In fact, I only received it from him once in my whole life. But when that day came and he spoke those magical words, they would prove to be as beautiful and impactful as this young kid could have ever imagined.

No matter how small or insignificant others may find this childhood story, I know the effect it had on me and how it changed the course of my competitive life. When I say I had a *burning desire to win* and that I carried it with me throughout my career, I am being as sincere as I can be. My dad didn't just teach this; he welded it into me. Whether or not he intended to do it doesn't matter. What matters is that it was now part of who I was as a person and as an athlete. This trial by fire during my critical developmental years would later help me in the Arena because of the timeless lessons it taught me.

I learned that respect had to be earned, and even when earned, it may not be given. I learned that no matter how hard you try, sometimes it still may not be enough to win. I learned that if you don't want to get mocked and humiliated, you have to do something about it. I learned that every time you enter an Arena, you better bring your A-game or face the real possibility of getting your ass kicked. Finally, I learned that I didn't like losing because losing meant more "disrespect" from my father, and that was a pain I would avoid at all costs.

• • •

In total, a seed had been planted inside of my soul, and it said winning was important. Throughout my career, this would be a critical source of motivation and the driving force that guided me in the Arena. Call it whatever you want, I call it the "burning desire to win," and now that I was entering high school, this *intangible gift* would prove to be a good thing to have.

Dad and me in the back yard. Notice I had a baseball in my right hand. My father was tough, stern, and to the point. He was also my hero.

My baby sister Rhonda and me.

Playing catch with my dad in the backyard and it's pretty obvious there was no place I'd rather be.

Mother, Rhonda, and me in 1969.

"Don't mess with my little sister." Rhonda and me as kids.

Here you have the starting pitcher for the mighty Richards Sporting Goods little league team.

Chapter 2

THE JOURNEY BEGINS

Only those who risk going too far can possibly find out how far they can go. —T.S. ELIOT

THE SUMMER before my freshman year in high school, my parents moved our family across town, which, unfortunately for me, meant finding new friends and attending a high school I knew nothing about. Westlake High School in Austin, Texas, is better known today than it was back in the fall of 1976. Now famous for its football program, which produced the likes of Super Bowl champion quarterback Nick Foles, University of Texas star QB Sam Elhinger, Justin Tucker, the most accurate field goal kicker in NFL history, and of course, future NFL Hall of Famer Drew Brees, the Chaparrals are now recognized on a national level. When I arrived on campus though, things were a little more scaled back. Granted, the Chaps were still very good in sports (and my class would produce two professional athletes), but for the most part, Westlake was just a young, medium-sized school on the outskirts of the capital city. I played both basketball and baseball, having given up football a few years earlier because every coach wanted to make me a lineman—a position that simply didn't fit me. Basketball was my true love, and it wasn't even close. I figured if I were going to fit in at my new school, I would have to do it on the basketball court, so this lanky fourteen-year-old set out to do just that.

I have never been an outgoing person; it's just not who I am. Unfortunately, this made it difficult to make new friends. I was seen as aloof and somewhat of a loner. As high school began, I rode the bus to campus each morning and headed straight to the gym. Every day, by myself, I practiced basketball until the first morning bell. This became my daily routine. As luck would have it, I was riding a growth spurt that began about a year earlier and was now 6′2″ and 170 pounds. Needless to say, it didn't take long for the basketball coaches to notice the solitary kid who was always working on his game. Soon after that, I befriended a group of like-minded guys to join me on my morning gym routine and eventually found myself starting on a pretty salty freshman team. I enjoyed this experience immensely. By the end of the first semester, I had established roots, made friends, and knew I had found a home at Westlake High School.

With three games left in the freshman basketball season, I came down awkwardly on my ankle. In the days that followed, the coaches kept me in the trainer's room, alternating heat and ice in an effort to get me on the court. At game time, my ankle was taped tight, and fortunately, I didn't miss a beat, finishing the season on the court with my teammates for what would be (up to that point) the best sports experience of my life. I loved high school more than I could have ever imagined, and now that the basketball season was over, it was on to baseball. Had it been up to me, I would have played basketball year-round, but our season was over and baseball tryouts were underway, so I gladly went.

For the record, I liked baseball, but I didn't love it. Now don't get me wrong. I played a lot of baseball and pitched for a Babe Ruth team that won a state championship, so I don't want to give the false impression that baseball was meaningless to me—it just wasn't my passion. After participating in the first baseball practice, the coach noticed me limping while running laps and wanted to know what the situation was. I told him I would be fine. After three days of this, he told me that I would no longer be able to practice until I was checked out by a doctor. Having no choice, I went in for X-rays, and sure enough, they discovered that my basketball injury from three weeks earlier was actually a broken ankle. Just like that, my baseball season was over before I threw a single pitch. I was done with sports for the rest of the year and a little bitter, to say the least.

I entered my sophomore year with anticipation and high hopes. By then, I was socially and athletically established and felt secure in my surroundings. I was a starter on the JV basketball team and had developed into a pretty good player. I was now 6′3″ and 180 pounds, and for a kid my size, had good touch on the ball. There's no doubt that endless hours of playing ping-pong had helped develop my hand-eye coordination. Now granted, there were a lot of kids at the school who had great coordination, but they were usually not my size, which became a real advantage. The basketball season was again enjoyable, and when it ended, I was really looking forward to baseball since I never got my chance the year before. The high school scene no longer overwhelmed me, and I had a genuine sense of confidence going into the tryouts. I felt I had something to prove, that I belonged, and wasn't intimidated by the older players. With that said, I mean no disrespect to the upperclassmen who were very good. All I am saying is that my mindset going in was that the coaches were going to pick the best players for varsity, and I was determined to prove that I was one of them, without regard to anyone else's status.

After tryouts, the coaches announced that I had made the varsity team. I wasn't the only sophomore who made the team that year. Kelly Gruber, who would go on to play nine years in the major leagues, win a Golden Glove, and become a two-time Major League Baseball All-Star, was on the varsity team as well. Kelly was a phenomenal athlete who also played basketball, in addition to being the football team's star quarterback. As the season got underway and I was given my first start, I never really felt any pressure. Like I said, basketball was my real passion, baseball was just for fun, and

I played it that way. It also didn't hurt that I was only a sophomore who entered the season completely under the radar. In those days, Westlake didn't have any devices capable of gauging the speed of a pitch, but I'm pretty confident that I could hit close to 90 mph on my fastball. By the time district play began, I was the number one pitcher on the staff. We won district and made it to the regionals, and I finished the season with a 14–3 record. Little did I know at the time, pro scouts had been coming to watch me play, and little did they know, basketball was still my favorite sport. Oh well.

For better or worse, everything I said earlier about my father is accurate. What I didn't mention is that as hard as he was, there is no doubt he wanted me to do well, despite the fact that he would never say it. Growing up, there was never a time that I asked him to throw with me, and he said no. Not once! It didn't matter how tired or stressed he was. If I asked him, he would get up, go out to our back-yard, and throw with me. The man knew very little about baseball, so he wasn't really my coach, but he took the time to throw with me, and that not only helped me develop, it meant the world. I distinctly remember how he put his glove in a certain position and told me to hit it. Never missing an opportunity to impress him, I'd put it right where he asked. We'd do this again and again, which, over the years, accumulated into countless hours. Without a doubt, that is how I developed both my arm strength and accuracy, and were it not for him, that would have never happened. What's more, my father never missed a single game. He wouldn't say anything before or after, but he never missed a game.

As my junior year rolled around, it all began to click for me. I was now 6′4″ and weighed 190 pounds. I made the varsity basketball team, including the starting lineup. As a team, the stars had aligned for us, and our coach, Dent Taylor, would field a team that was the best Westlake had ever seen. Coach Taylor was one of the many exceptional coaches for whom I had the privilege to play under. He instilled discipline, developed his players, and was a master at the X's and O's. Our team had it all—height, shooting, ball handling, and we could run. This was an exciting time for me because I finally got to compete at a high level in a game that I loved. To say I was in heaven would be an understatement.

The season went much as expected. We won district, and it seemed no team could beat us. I was averaging fourteen points and twelve rebounds per game, and as a team, we were averaging an impressive seventy-five points per game. We steamrolled our way to the playoffs and, at one point, were riding an eighteen-game winning streak. We made it to the regional finals. But unfortunately, we got a bad draw, which forced us to face Huntsville, who was not only ranked No. 1 in Texas, Class 3A, but had also (earlier that season) beaten the No. 1 Class 4A team above us. We felt we were the No. 2 team in the state, and so did many others, so this matchup should have taken place in the state tournament finals. Regardless of how we may have felt, this is not how it worked. We happened to be in their region, and we would have to play them earlier than we would have liked. It was that simple. We played them hard, but in the end, we lost 55–42. Their defense was so disruptive that they kept us thirty-three points under our season average. They were better, no doubt, but it was still a hard pill to swallow. We finished the season at 28–2.

When basketball season ended, I again went directly to baseball, but this time things would feel much different than they had before. For starters, we had a new coach, and this guy would change the dynamics of Westlake baseball. Coach Howard Bushong was incredible. Remember when I spoke of the importance of a good coach? With Bushong, we got one. Believe it or not, he didn't teach me mechanics, as that was really not the practice back then. What he did teach was the mental side of baseball and which pitches should be thrown in particular situations. It may seem pretty simple, but it isn't, and he was a master at getting points across in such a way that I could understand them. A new coach wasn't the only change that occurred that year. It also became readily apparent that I was no longer the young kid who came out of nowhere and surprised everyone. People knew me now, and with that came expectations, and with expectations came pressure. I could no longer ride the coattails of a lanky sophomore pitcher who achieved more than anyone expected. The spotlight had found me, and for the first time in my life, I would have to deal with notoriety. Even more significant is that I began to love the game of baseball, and when you really care about something, it increases the internal pressure to do it better. Things were definitely different, and if I wanted to have a good year, I would have to navigate a new mental minefield. Understanding and managing newfound pressures was certainly a challenge, but thankfully, I had help. First, I had talented teammates who had each other's backs. Secondly, I had an incredible coach who understood the dynamics of pressure and always knew how to instill calmness in the eye of the storm. Finally, I had that ever-present and deeply rooted desire to win. This gift would focus and guide me every time I took the mound. The complexities and pressures of the new season were challenging, but I was eager to get it started and face a new unknown.

As a team, and on paper, we were better than the year before. The buzz around the Westlake community was that this team could make it all the way to the state tournament. We started the season fast, and with every win, the team grew in confidence. It appeared that we were everything as advertised and I couldn't have been more excited. Unfortunately for me, the excitement was fleeting as my world came crashing down inside a south Texas hotel room. We had been playing well at a tournament in Uvalde, and after the first day's games, we retreated to the hotel to rest up for the next day. My father, who was staying at the same hotel, called and asked me to come over to his room. As I entered, I immediately noticed that he was visibly shaken. There was an unsettling silence as I just stood there and as he fumbled for the courage to speak. Then, it came out. He told me that he had just gotten off the phone with a doctor in Austin and that my younger sister, Rhonda, had been diagnosed with cancer. Choking back tears, he said that it was very serious and that she would require surgery within a week. Watching my stoic and hardened father reduced to tears and hearing that my little sister was in serious trouble was like getting hit with a sledgehammer. I was confused and stunned, but I knew one thing, I had to get back to Austin to see her. After a long and painful discussion with my father, he insisted, against my wishes, that I stay with the team and finish out the tournament. I obeyed my father.

When I returned to Austin, I couldn't think of anything except the well-being of my sister. Rhonda is two years younger than me, and we are very close. She is sweet, gifted, and kind—and anyone who knows her or spent time around her would tell you the same. The very thought of losing her was overwhelming. In the days and weeks that followed, my father was adamant that I remain with the team and maintain my daily routine. His was not the reaction of some psycho sports dad who wanted to ensure that his son kept his name in the spotlight. No, this was an endearing decision made by a father who loved his son and wanted to protect him as best he could from the circumstances which had besieged us. Dad knew that being around my teammates and coach was the best thing for me, and in hindsight, he was right.

The date of my sister's surgery had been set, and it coincided with a game I was slated to pitch. Of course, Coach Bushong understood that I would be at the hospital with my sister, but my father didn't see it that way. He told me there was nothing that I could do sitting in a waiting room and that if I wanted to do something meaningful, I should go out and pitch the game in her honor, then see her after the game. He was right, and that's exactly what I did. Motivated by the thought of my sister, I pitched a real gem. It was a no-hitter, and if it weren't for me walking the very last batter, it would have been a perfect game. On the mound that night, I felt a sense of focus and purpose I had never experienced before, and this would arguably become the best game I ever pitched. I will always be proud of the way I performed that night in her honor, and like Dad promised, I left the game immediately afterward and went to see Rhonda, who was just coming out of a successful surgery. At the hospital, I presented her with the game ball, and there wasn't a dry eye in the room. She knew I was thinking about her, and I'm confident that helped lift her spirits. I will never forget that moment and will always appreciate my father for asking me to play that game for her. He made that moment possible.

The road for Rhonda was difficult. The chemotherapy was brutal, and watching her hug the toilet all day was more than my parents and I could bear. It was especially hard on my mother, who had to endure watching her beloved daughter suffer through this. No mother should have to go through that, and having to witness the pain that both she and my sister were going through was extremely difficult for me. The fight Rhonda displayed throughout this time changed me forever, and to this day, it helps me put life's events into their proper perspective. Rhonda would fight and beat cancer two more times, and in each instance, demonstrate the same resilience and inspiring will to live that most people are never fortunate enough to witness. She is a fighter, a winner, and more importantly, the most beautiful person you'd ever want to meet. Today, Rhonda lives cancer-free in Hawaii with her family, where she teaches first grade. Although physically separated by thousands of miles, we remain very close.

My junior baseball season marched on, and thoughts of my little sister never left my mind. She was proud of her older brother, and watching me play brought her joy at a time when there was little joy to be found. This made it easy for me to continue to play because I was now playing for her. We finished the season as district champs and had high expectations of making it to state.

• • •

Despite the trauma that had descended upon my family that season, there was one positive. College recruiters and pro scouts were now present every time I took the mound, and they weren't just there for me. By this time, Kelly Gruber was attracting national attention as well. Our games began to take on a circus-like atmosphere, where we consistently played to packed houses and in front of fifteen to twenty scouts and recruiters. This was a pleasant distraction at a time when I desperately needed one. The team would eventually make it to the regionals, where we lost to a Cleburne squad that was headlined by a phenomenal shortstop named Spike Owen. As disappointing as the loss was, Cleburne had the better team, and we would have to wait another year to try and get it done. I finished the season with a 13–1 record and was named district MVP and All-State. There was, however, no celebration for me, as these honors rang hollow in a year that I'd just as soon forget.

Going up and under for the score. I loved every minute I was on the basketball court.

Westlake had a really good team my junior year.

I made the varsity team as a sophomore, and baseball was beginning to be my passion.

My beautiful sister Rhonda. Her cancer diagnosis during my junior year turned our lives upside down. She never gave up and won the fight. We are still very close.

Chapter 3

IT'LL LAST FOREVER

*In all my years of coaching, I've never seen a high school kid
who was as fierce or intimidating as Calvin Schiraldi
was when he was on the mound.*
—HOWARD BUSHONG, Westlake Baseball Coach

AS MY SENIOR YEAR ARRIVED, Rhonda was doing better, and I felt like I had a new lease on life. I was now 6′5″, weighed 205 pounds, and was a seasoned veteran in high school basketball and baseball. As the basketball season rolled around, I could barely contain my excitement. I was coming off a really good junior year and knew that with another year of development, I would be one of the area's better basketball players. Unfortunately, I knew, and I think Coach Taylor did too, that the basketball team would not be as dominant. We had simply graduated too many good players to maintain the level of play achieved the year prior. As usual, Coach Taylor got the most out of us, and we made it to the postseason but lost by one point in the early playoff rounds. Even had we won that game, I doubt we would have made it much further. The teams that year were just better than we were. I finished the year averaging twenty points and thirteen rebounds and was named first team All-Central Texas. I was proud of the player that I had become and cherished every moment spent on the court, but my basketball career had come to an end. I could have played at a smaller college, but I wanted to play Division 1, and I simply wasn't good enough for that. Basketball helped me get acclimated to a brand new school where I didn't know a soul. The sport taught me how to compete and what teamwork is all about. It also kept me in shape for baseball. I will forever be grateful to this sport and to Coach Taylor for giving me the joy and knowledge this wonderful game brought me. As hard as it was to accept, I knew that I had to say goodbye and move on. Fortunately, there was baseball, and the anticipation and enthusiasm surrounding our team were contagious. There was no other way to say it: we were loaded, and everybody knew it. I was as excited as everyone else but faced a problem in the form of a stubborn illness that put my entire senior season in jeopardy.

With two weeks to go in the basketball season, I contracted a serious strain of strep, which led to a severe gum infection. It was so bad that I couldn't eat and had to go on a liquid diet which lasted weeks. Being that I kept playing basketball during this time, the weight started falling off of my body. Before the illness ran its course, I lost twenty-five pounds and had to enter the baseball season a physical shell of my former self. This was not good, and I knew it.

Much like my junior year basketball squad, the stars had aligned for this senior season baseball team, and Coach Bushong was the perfect guy to lead us. Not only did he understand winning, he had masterfully developed this group for the moment we faced. The expectations were incredibly high, and the Westlake community was just as excited as we were. Games continued to have a circus-like atmosphere, with scouts and recruiters peppered throughout the stands trying to get a look at Kelly and me. However, it was evident that the weight loss had cost me precious mph on my fastball, and I was going to have to fight my way through it. It was frustrating as hell but proved to be just another of the many things in my life that challenged me in unexpected ways, only to make me stronger in the end.

The team started hot, developing an aura that the only team who could beat us was us. Well, it wasn't long before that actually happened. Only a few games into the season, I was on the mound in a tournament. It was the bottom half of the last inning, and we had a 2–1 lead, with bases loaded and one out. The batter hit a ground ball back to me, which I fielded cleanly, and now all I needed to do was throw it to the catcher, who would then throw it to first for the double play to end the game. Pretty simple, right? We'd done it a thousand times in practice, but in this instance, it didn't turn out that way. After fielding the ball, I immediately threw it home as I was supposed to, but I threw it about ten feet over the catcher's head, where it hit the backstop with a loud thud. Chaos ensued, two runs scored, the game was over, and I was left standing on the mound like a complete dumb ass. Gone was the game, and gone was my chance at an unblemished senior season. Needless to say, it was a very long and painful bus ride home.

Thankfully, things returned to being really good in a short amount of time. In the weeks that followed, I threw two no-hitters and several shutouts despite my severe weight loss, which by the way, I wouldn't regain until my junior year in college. I had found a way to compensate for the lost weight and was beginning to hit my stride.

My mother loved watching me play, and I felt that every time I took the field. In late March, we played a game on a pretty cold afternoon, and she wore a black wool dress to be comfortable. I pitched extremely well that day and because of that, she decided to wear that wool dress to every game in a superstitious attempt to keep me playing well. These were special times for me, and her encouragement and support really meant something.

As a team, we kept winning and seemed to get better with each outing. We won district, and more importantly, we won our first several playoff games. Then it was on to the regional finals, which had been a roadblock for us the past two years. Getting through this stretch would mean a trip to the state championships, but standing in our way was a best out of three series with Brenham, an established Texas powerhouse. Our coach made it clear that this was our time, and he never let us lose sight of that. I pitched and won the first game of the series, we barely lost game two, and I returned to the mound for game three. I was pitching a good game, not great, but also hit a home run, which certainly helped my cause. We took a 5–1 lead to the last inning, and I knew what was on the line and wanted nothing more than to end this thing and get our coach and his team to state. Three outs later, it happened. We punched our ticket to state, celebrating like we had never done before. Westlake High School was going to the Texas State Championship Baseball Tournament, and the feeling was like nothing I had ever known.

To his credit, Coach Bushong didn't let the celebration last long. He wasn't satisfied with us just being there and made damn sure we weren't either. He knew the importance of this moment and how extremely rare this opportunity was. Simply put, he wasn't going to let us be satisfied with anything other than a state title. By this time, the team was seasoned, gritty, and mentally tough. We arrived at the state tourney with a singular focus, and although we definitely felt the pressure, we knew we belonged. The tournament was a simple format: four teams in the semi-finals playing a single game with the winners vying for the state championship—also in a single game. Our first outing was against Snyder, and Coach Bushong put me on the mound. We jumped on them early and were up 7–0 after a few innings. I had thrown just forty-eight pitches, and Coach pulled me to save my arm for the championship game. We went on to win the game, and now laying in front of us, and within our grasp, was the shining pot of high school gold. Years of toil and heartache would be our power source as we entered the Arena to fight one last time together for the ultimate prize. It would not be easy. Our obstacle would be an immensely talented DeSoto team who were not only the defending state champs but also the current No. 1 ranked team in Texas. They were battle-tested veterans of the state tournament, so any thought of them being intimidated by us or this atmosphere was quickly dismissed. The table was set for a clash between two high school powerhouses, and the stakes couldn't be higher.

I recall being very nervous before this game, but I wasn't overwhelmed. Coach Bushong had always believed in me, and this trust gave me confidence. What also gave me confidence was my experience. By now, I had been in the pressure cooker for three years and had developed a game I knew I could rely on. My weight loss was the only factor that kept me from being perfectly prepared, yet despite that, I had played enough games at this new weight to understand it, and there was no doubt I was as ready for this moment. In the locker room before the game, Coach Bushong told us, "If you perform today the way I know you're capable of, I can promise you, it'll last forever."

As I stood in front of the dugout, looking at a packed house of over 5,000 spectators, I saw my mother in the stands, wearing her black wool dress on a very hot, Texas summer day. It made me smile. My father was sitting next to her, and as our eyes met, a slight grin appeared on his stoic face, exposing the pride he could no longer conceal. I then turned my attention towards the field and the fact that this would be my last game in a Westlake uniform. I was determined to give everything I had for the school and team I had grown to love.

The game itself was unbelievable. It was a dogfight from the beginning, with both teams showing an unyielding desire to be champions—neither of us would go away. We jumped out to a 2-0 lead in the top half of the first, and then I took the mound. I felt good out there, but I couldn't find the strike zone to save my life and was walking batters left and right. At one point, I walked four batters in a row. Of course, I felt that the strike zone was a little tight, and I remember being unhappy about it. In reality, I just wasn't getting them out. After I walked the fifth batter of the inning, Coach Bushong came to the mound with the possible intent of pulling me from the game. I remember distinctly telling him; not a chance and to get the hell out of here. Coach and I had been in the trenches together for two years now, and he knew I meant no disrespect. I was just simply expressing to him, in the heat of the moment, that I was okay—he kept me in. When I finally ended the inning with a strikeout, it was time to assess the damage. Six runs had scored, and I had walked five batters. My first inning pitch count was through the roof, and we were down 6–2. I had dug our team into a deep hole at the wrong time and against the wrong opponent. With that said, I settled down nicely after the first, and we clawed our way back, even taking the lead. The resilience of my teammates was awe-inspiring; they had my back all the way, and I played off of it. As the game moved into the late innings, my pitch count was really high, and if you include the forty-eight pitches I had thrown the day before, it was really, really high. Coach Bushong kept a watchful eye, but he knew me, and he also knew there was not a chance in hell I was going to leave that game. Scheduled for seven innings, regulation ended without a champion being crowned. This back and forth masterpiece, painted by two relentless high school teams, was headed for extra innings, tied at nine. Our bats came alive in the top of the eighth, and we scored two runs—this was big on many levels. In the bottom half, up 11–9, they scored one run, and I was facing a situation where we had one out with the tying run on third.

Despite the ridiculous amount of pitches thrown, I felt great and was actually throwing harder in the extra inning than in the earlier ones. I was two batters away from ending this thing, but I knew that time was running out, and I wouldn't be able to do this much longer—no matter how good I felt. I struck out the first guy in three pitches, leaving us one out away. I quickly got two strikes on the next batter, and with my 189th pitch of the game, struck him out.

A glorious dogpile ensued.

At the bottom of that pile was a physically and emotionally drained athlete who could proudly say he gave everything he had. The game was epic; we crawled our way out of the hole I had dug and finished it off in Texas high school baseball's biggest Arena. We were state champions, having reached the pinnacle of a game that we all so passionately loved. What's more, we did it for a coach who clearly deserved the distinction of being called a State Champion. The stands were chaotic, with our crowd jumping, screaming, and going absolutely nuts. Never in my wildest dreams could I have imagined how this would feel, and little did I know the best was yet to come. As officials cleared the field and the celebration was drawing down, I found myself alone by the dugout fence, reflecting on what had just happened and taking in the moment as best I could. I was drenched in sweat and emotionally numb, with my body shaking all over. I couldn't feel my right arm. That's when I saw my father coming toward me. As our eyes met, he walked up, shook my hand, and said, "You did a good job out there, Calvin. I'm really proud of you." The words I had longed to hear since I was a child had finally come, and the feeling it gave me was everything I had always imagined it would be. I will never forget that moment as long as I live.

The Westlake community went crazy, and we were treated like rock stars. Coach Bushong was right in not being satisfied with just getting there because he knew that winning a state championship is something no one can ever take away from you. He promised us it would last a lifetime, and it has. I finished my senior year with an 18–1 record, and to this day, I'm haunted by that boneheaded throw I made in the earlier game, which blew a perfect season. I was named district MVP for the second year in a row and made the All-State Team. I was also heralded by many sports outlets as the top high school pitcher in the state of Texas. Years later, I would have my jersey retired by the school. Please note, I apologize for using "I" and "me" in this text and want to make it clear that I fully recognize that none of this happened without my teammates and coaches—none of it. I say this sincerely and without reservation. Any accolades I ever received belong as much to them as they do to me. With that said, having my jersey retired by the school was an incredible honor, especially considering the role Westlake played in molding me.

As the tenth overall pick in the 1980 Major League draft, Kelly Gruber was drafted out of high school by the Cleveland Indians and went on to have a stellar career with the Toronto Blue Jays. Westlake would appropriately retire his jersey as well. Coach Bushong would later be quoted as saying, "No matter how long I stay in coaching, I doubt I will ever coach a team again that has two athletes the caliber of Kelly Gruber and Calvin Schiraldi." This was quite a compliment coming from a man who had given me so much. As for my future, I was headed to The University of Texas to play for legendary coach Cliff Gustafson. It was a dream come true, and I was thrilled at the opportunity that stood before me.

. . .

As I close this chapter, I want to say—without apology—that winning was always my driving force. If winning isn't the final goal, I don't see the point of playing the game. Yes, it's extremely difficult. It's also elusive. But above all, winning challenges every aspect of your mental, physical and emotional being. Those who seek victory do so at their own peril because losing is, at best, extremely unpleasant, and at its worst, traumatic. This is why my high school experiences are so important to me. I entered Westlake with the desire to win and left with the understanding of *how* to win. By the time I graduated, and despite the fact that I was still a teenager, I was a battle-tested veteran of the Arena. In those three years of baseball, I walked off the mound having never lost a district game (28–0). I had three no-hitters, a dozen shutouts, forty-five wins, a state championship, and was considered one of the top high school pitchers in the nation. These accomplishments were a combination of outstanding coaching, talented teammates, and the fact that every time I entered the Arena, I did so armed with a burning desire to leave it a winner. Considering everything that had transpired, it's hard to imagine that just four years earlier, I was an intimidated fourteen-year-old kid riding the bus to a school I knew nothing about. My days on that campus not only shaped me competitively, they changed me in ways that would last forever. But bigger stages and far greater challenges now awaited me. My new Arena would be college baseball and my new team, the Texas Longhorns. I couldn't wait to get started.

Pitching in a game my senior year at Westlake. This team really got on a roll.

Kelly and me relaxing after practice. Pro scouts and recruiters were routine for every game.

"IT'LL LAST FOREVER"

Celebrating the strike out that won the state championship against DeSoto. There was no feeling like it.

Chapter 4

HOOK 'EM

Character cannot be developed in ease and quiet. Only through experience of trial and suffering can the soul be strengthened, ambition inspired, and success achieved. —HELEN KELLER

MY HOMETOWN of Austin, Texas, is one of the most unique places in the entire country. It's known for its natural beauty, live music scene, superb restaurants, and most of all, The University of Texas Longhorns. When I arrived on campus in the fall of 1980, Austin was less than half the size it is now, which made it the perfect college town. Although it had plenty of sports fans, Austin didn't have a professional team like other major cities. This meant UT athletics held a monopoly on the sports entertainment market. Football was king, but UT baseball was one of the top programs in the country and had carved out a significant niche of its own. With this niche came a large, loyal, and very passionate fan base decked out in burnt orange, flashing their extended pinky and index fingers and shouting, "Hook 'Em, Horns!"

There was a buzz around Austin centered on baseball coach Cliff Gustafson's latest recruiting class. Remarkably, this class was headlined by the top four high school pitchers in Texas. It's not unique that these four committed to UT since attracting top talent there was not unusual. The truly remarkable thing is that Coach Gus didn't lose any of them to the Major League draft, which is a highly common occurrence for top prospects. I was one of these four recruits, and I can tell you first hand that we garnered a lot of attention from the very moment we set foot on the 40 Acres (a favored term used to describe the UT campus). Needless to say, this made my transition to college a helluva lot easier than the one into high school, and I knew in my heart that I was right where I needed to be.

The message above the door in the Texas baseball locker room was simple but very clear. It read, "The winning traditions of The University of Texas will not be entrusted to the timid or weak." I recall seeing this for the first time on a recruiting trip, and it sent chills down my spine. We've all seen fancy slogans hanging in locker rooms saying shit like "Champions live here," "Give it everything you have," or "Leave it on the field." More often than not, these are just platitudes that take up space in an environment not worthy of having them exhibited. I can assure you that the words that hung in our locker room were not platitudes. They laid out an unyielding message as to what the expectations would be for those who represented The University of Texas. Furthermore, our coach would serve as judge and jury to see that this message was adhered to. Cliff Gustafson couldn't have been more different than Howard Bushong at Westlake. The main difference between the two was in the way they handled their players. Coach Bushong was more of a player's coach, light-hearted, and pleasant to be around. Coach Gus was not. He was a stern disciplinarian, intolerant of mediocrity, and personified the "My way or the highway" approach to coaching. I didn't always agree with his methods, but his record spoke for itself, and who the hell was I anyway to question anything about him? Gus was a perennial winner on the national stage who had dominated the Southwest Conference and made a home for his teams at the College World Series. He created an atmosphere around the program that embodied those words in the locker room. Anyone who didn't act accordingly with strict adherence to the message was shown the door. It was that simple.

When fall practice began, the first thing I noticed was that the talent level was like nothing I had ever seen. All of the pitchers could throw, all of the hitters could hit, and there was speed everywhere. Watching these athletes was like having a bucket of ice water thrown in your face, and it rudely awakened me to the fact that my days of being Mr. High School Badass were officially over. Nobody gave a shit about what you had done in the past; it was all meaningless now, and the slate of past accomplishments was wiped clean like they never happened. As if competing against this jaw-dropping pool of talent wasn't enough, what made things worse was that there were two lingering issues with my body that kept me from being one hundred percent. First, I still hadn't put the weight back on from my high school illness. I felt fine, but I just couldn't seem to put on weight. Second, my arm still hadn't recovered from the state tournament, where I had thrown 237 pitches in a two-day stretch. There was no structural damage or anything like that; I just couldn't seem to get the same zing out of a pitch that I was accustomed to. I was throwing between 85–88 mph (maybe), and against these guys, that was going to be an issue. I fully understood that this was my problem and mine alone and that I had better figure it out or I wouldn't be around for long. A sobering reality had set in—this was big-time college baseball, which meant leaving your excuses and your little league trophies with your mother back home because nobody here gave a rat's ass about either one.

As for the team, freshmen hung out with each other because the older guys basically snubbed our asses. In fact, they wouldn't even call us by our names. They dubbed me "Nibbler" because of the way I could paint the corners of the strike zone or "nibble" away at it. There were also all kinds of established traditions designed to make the freshmen as uncomfortable as possible. The mindset was that freshmen weren't worthy of being around the program or the more established players, and until we earned it, they would treat us like shit. Early on, there was one initiation that we would have to endure, and afterward, would essentially gain some acceptance. The upperclassmen announced the date for this "fun packed" event and taunted us for days regarding the misery they intended to put us through. There was one problem, though. This freshmen group was determined to not partake in the festivities.

The night of the initiation, we had strict orders to be in our room at exactly 7:00pm and wait for the veteran players to arrive. Instead, we gathered a basket of eggs and hid at the top of Moore Hill, overlooking our dorm. We knew that the upperclassmen would be on time because they were hell-bent on giving the freshman their just due. We sat patiently, waiting to ambush, and sure enough, they came, marching with purpose toward our dorm. In a flash, from the top of the hill, all hell broke loose. Eight collegiate baseball players hurling eggs with pinpoint accuracy into a group of unsuspecting fools. It was an awesome sight watching this panicked group of initiators scattering for cover with egg yoke dripping all over them. Of course, we knew that this act of aggression toward our "superiors" was going to cost us, but we wanted to send a message that this freshmen group was a little different. Well, as it turned out, sending that message kind of worked—and it kind of didn't.

The next day at practice, an upperclassman told me that he was impressed with the balls it took to pull off the attack from Moore Hill, but then, with a shit-eating grin on his face, he explained that we were to be in our room that night at seven o'clock or we would regret it for the rest of our lives. This time, we had no choice, and they were right; it was as miserable as they said it would be. When they arrived at our dorm, the first thing they made us do was go outside and elephant walk around campus while singing "the Eyes of Texas." With beautiful coeds watching and laughing as we paraded by, this scene not only brought our egos back in check, it managed to shred every ounce of dignity we thought we had. They then blindfolded us, put us in a car, and drove us to the woods located who the hell knows where. We were then removed from the car and put in a line where they made us pass a raw egg from one guy to the other—with our mouths. What's worse, the last guy had to swallow it. Then they peppered our bare legs with BB guns (which stung like hell), but it seemed to bring immense joy to them. Next, those sorry bastards got back in the car and drove off. It was dark by then, and we had no idea where we were. I remember thinking at the time that maybe the ambush at Moore Hill wasn't such a good idea after all. When we finally made our way back in the early morning hours of the next day, the initiation was over. We were now part of the team. In the end, I think they appreciated the moxie we showed with the egg assault, but whether they did or not, we had earned the respect of our "superiors" and were now officially in the club. Looking back, it was all a pretty good time.

Gaining respect from the upperclassmen was one thing, but getting it from Coach Gus would be an entirely different undertaking. Especially since all four of the pitchers from this heralded freshman class were struggling, and Coach was kind enough to point it out every chance he got. The freshman pitchers were Mike Capel, Bobby Hinson, John Manchin, and me. John would leave after his freshman year to attend a junior college, and Bobby would transfer to Lubbock Christian University following his sophomore year. I remember how difficult these times were for all of us. Even though we had been very accomplished high school players with big arms, the fact remained that we were still teenagers. This sink or swim environment was difficult to navigate, and at times, could be depressing. One afternoon, following a mediocre practice by the freshman pitchers, Coach Gus demanded an on-field pitchers' meeting. He individually destroyed us all, and his mother would have been appalled by the way he chose to describe us. After verbally assaulting the others, Gus finally got around to me, saying, "And you, Schiraldi. Do you not realize that I can pull your scholarship any time I want to? If you think your time here is guaranteed, you are sadly mistaken."

This was a deeply troubling message at a time where I was struggling and didn't have an answer as to why. At this moment, I felt the same sense of hopelessness I did as a child when I was facing off against my father in table sports. Like then, I was wondering how in the world I could do this. The task in front of me was so daunting that I didn't even know where to begin. I left practice dejected, demoralized and humiliated, but I knew I wasn't going to quit, and more importantly, I knew that I didn't like the way that any of this felt. I was determined to find my way back to the success I once knew and was willing to do whatever it took. I just wasn't quite sure how.

I ended my freshman year with very limited playing time and an underwhelming 2–2 record. The team, however, was really good, and we made it to the College World Series in Omaha, Nebraska. Omaha was amazing, and Rosenblatt Stadium provided the perfect venue. I was allowed to travel with the team but didn't get to suit up, which was yet another in the long line of humbling experiences I had to endure that season. The sad fact was I had the entire year to prove I could help this team win, and yet, I didn't do it. Because of that, I had to watch my teammates play without me. Although I was very supportive and energetic, being a cheerleader didn't sit well with me. Despite it all, there's no denying that being with the team at the College World Series was an exciting time. The atmosphere surrounding the Series was like no other. The people of Omaha were wonderful, and they all knew and appreciated the game. The baseball talent on display was astounding, and it was a real treat watching these athletes vie for the National Championship. Our team reached the semifinals and ended the season with a 58–9 record. That whirlwind year went by in a flash and left me with two distinct takeaways. One, I didn't like the contempt shown towards me by Coach Gus, and if I wanted that to change, I had to get better. Two, I loved every single thing about Omaha, and I was passionate about returning there—only next time, as a player.

Playing summer ball was a necessity for Division 1 baseball players, and at Texas, you couldn't survive unless you did. Getting a break from school and Coach Gus proved to be a good thing for me. I was assigned to a team in Liberal, Kansas, and arrived there with all of the knowledge I had acquired during my freshman year. These leagues were no step-down, mind you; they were loaded with top-tier, Division 1 talent. Playing here would turn out to be critical for me in a multitude of ways. I had a lot to reconcile in my head, not the least of which was to become mentally tougher. As the games began and the summer progressed, things would begin to click for me again, and the game slowed down to where I could think clearly and play more relaxed. The surroundings were now less daunting, and I was at a comfort level that I hadn't experienced since high school. With each outing, my confidence grew, and I began to dominate from the mound like I had in those earlier years. I finished summer ball and left Kansas with much more than an 8–1 record. I left as a better version of myself. The entire year came together for me that summer, and everything made more sense. Not only would I be returning to Austin with my confidence fully restored, I would bring along an arm and a game that was ready to compete. It was time to show Coach Gus that he didn't make a mistake after all.

As the fall of my sophomore year arrived, there were several new players on the Texas roster, including two junior college transfers who would go on to make an immediate impact. One was a gifted catcher from California named Jeff Herron, and the other was a hard-throwing right-hander from Houston named Roger Clemens. Returning to the team was a solid pitching staff, exceptional hitters, and the best shortstop in the country, Spike Owen, who loved ribbing me about Cleburne High School knocking us out of the playoffs my junior year.

Position status at Texas was made or lost during the fall season. We scrimmaged every day, which would give Coach Gus an abundance of statistics from which to evaluate us. I had vastly improved coming into the fall, and my pitching coach, Clint Thomas, noticed right away. Thankfully, I spent most of my time under the guidance of Coach Thomas, who was skilled at teaching the art of pitching. Calm in demeanor and easy to talk to, Coach Thomas was instrumental in getting my game where it needed to be. I had a great fall campaign which propelled me to the starting rotation. On the surface, this didn't mean much, but to me, it meant a lot. I had spent the past eighteen months battling self-doubt, confusion, belittlement, an arm that wouldn't always cooperate. I got through all of this because I refused to concede, and at this particular moment, I was damn proud of that.

The guys were starting to bond, and one of our favorite pastimes was to go to a hangout near campus called Tricky Mickey's. The drinking age was eighteen back then, so none of us were skirting the law with fake IDs. Tricky Mickey's was lined with pool tables, and as you may recall from my childhood, I was real familiar with those surroundings. Mike Capel (who, by the way, also had an outstanding fall camp) and I loved to go there and shoot pool. Unbeknownst to the poor, unsuspecting souls inside the bar, I was practically raised on a billiard table. Mike was pretty good, too, and we sometimes held a table all night long, mowing down one team after another while money flowed into our pockets. It was quite the racket and a whole lot of fun. Playing pool wasn't all Tricky Mickey's offered. It also provided an escape from the grind of UT baseball, enabling us once or twice a week to be just like the other kids on campus. It was always packed, beautiful college girls were everywhere, and the drinks flowed all night. Football players made their home there as well, although we didn't hang around with them. The atmosphere and energy inside this club were incredible, and it became my go-to hangout throughout my college career. After a night at Mickey's, we'd head down the block and capped off the night with a double cheeseburger and fries. These were special times indeed.

As the 1982 baseball season got underway, I had clearly found my stride again. Two months into the schedule, I was 9–0, which included a one-hitter against highly ranked Wichita State University. Our Longhorn team was spectacular, by far the best team I had ever been on, and perhaps the best team I had ever seen. We began the season 33–0, which was one game shy of the all-time NCAA record. After winning the Southwest Conference, we went into the regional tournament as the number one ranked team in the nation, boasting an overall record of 54–4. The top four pitchers were Clemens, Capel, Killingsworth, and me, with a combined record of 35–2. Texas would host the regional tournament, and winning it meant a return trip to the College World Series in Omaha. It was a great time for our fans because they got to watch the college playoffs in their hometown, and as a team, we loved playing in front of them.

We began the tournament by winning our first game easily, and then Clemens threw a shutout against Oklahoma in Game 2. This was his third shutout in a row. Next, Capel and Killingsworth combined for a four-hit masterpiece in Game 3. Now, the only thing that stood between us and a ticket to the College World Series was a very scrappy Eastern Michigan team. Coach Gus put me on the mound, and the home crowd of 7,500 was electric. I threw six innings, gave up one run on six hits, and we won 9–1. We had rolled through Regionals in true championship fashion, and now it was off to Omaha, where this time, I'd be playing.

There is no way to properly describe what it was like to be a ballplayer at the College World Series in Omaha. I truly believe it is one of the best venues in all of sports. It offers a pure form of baseball, appreciated by true fans who know the game at a high level. Rosenblatt Stadium was not huge by any stretch, but its 14,000 seat capacity was perfectly suited for this event. When you pulled into town like we did with a 59–4 record and the consensus number one ranking, the target on our back could not have been any bigger. We were the team to beat—everyone knew it, and that in and of itself made this a more difficult proposition than it already was. Despite that, we were healthy, confident, and ready to show the world what all the fuss was about.

Roger Clemens started for us against the Oklahoma State Cowboys, who were ranked fourth in the nation. Clemens was having an exceptional year and was going into the game having pitched thirty-six consecutive scoreless innings, including three straight complete-game shutouts. Although he would give up a run in this game, it was still a masterful five-hit performance that we won 9–1. On to Round 2.

Our next opponent was perennial power, Stanford. Mike Capel, who was having a terrific year of his own, got the start. Stanford was an awesome team who showed no signs of being intimidated by us Longhorns. Mike lasted to the middle of the fifth inning, and with two men on, Coach Gus took him out and put me in. Being on the mound at Rosenblatt was a dream come true, but that dream turned into a nightmare almost immediately, as I gave up a three-run homer. As unsettling as that was, I didn't panic and retired fourteen of the next fifteen batters. Killingsworth replaced me in extra innings and closed out the game. We won a real nail-biter by a score of 8–6 and marched on to the third round.

The Miami Hurricanes were our next opponents, and they too were no strangers to the College World Series. Roger got the call and was the perfect guy to put up against them. The game was tight the entire way, and he would once again pitch a complete game—this time with seven hits scattered about. In any other situation, this would have been enough to win, something our hitters had proved time and again. But in this case, the Canes' pitching kept us in check, and we lost, 2–1. It was our first loss in nineteen games, but there was no time to sulk because one more loss meant we'd be going home.

We now found ourselves in the elimination bracket taking on the same Wichita State team that we had faced the previous spring. This was the team I had thrown a one-hit shutout against, and Coach Gus put me up to battle them again. Although I gave up a run in the top half of the first, I felt confident and in control. We countered their score with two runs of our own in the bottom half of the first to take the lead, 2–1. I held them scoreless in the second as they did us, so then it was onto the third. This was when, out of nowhere, the most unthinkable incident happened, which would shake my foundation for the foreseeable future.

Facing Kevin Penner, WSU's best hitter, I attempted an up-and-in fastball that completely got away from me and smashed into his face with a horrifying thud. Kevin was knocked out cold. A deafening silence fell over the crowd of 14,000, and for several minutes, you could hear a pin drop in that stadium as trainers attended to the motionless batter. The pitch had shattered his eye socket, and Penner had to be carted off the field and taken immediately to the hospital emergency room. Completely numb by this chain of events, I remember walking up and apologizing to him as he laid on the cart. I didn't know what else to do.

Now what? Over the years, I had faced plenty of turmoil on the mound and, in the middle of games, had to fight through waves of negative thoughts, but this was different. I had damn near killed this guy, and it was almost certain I had ended his promising career. I went back to the mound and desperately tried to regain my composure, but clearly, my efforts didn't work because I got my ass shelled. By the time Gus pulled me out of there, and the inning was over, the Shockers had scored six runs.

One minute I was in control of the game, and in a flash, I'm on the bench with my team, getting our asses handed to us by Wichita State. It was surreal, to say the least, and a troubling turn of events. Although we were now down 7–2, our hitters, true to form, got on base and threatened nearly every inning. However, we never could get them around. We went on to strand twelve base runners and eventually lost, 8–4. Just like that, our magical season was over, and I had never felt anything like this in my life. My third inning had cost this once–in–a–lifetime team a chance at the National Championship. Far worse, I had likely permanently injured a gifted young ballplayer in the process. How do you reconcile something like that? I couldn't—at least not for a very long time. After the game, I contacted the hospital to check on Kevin, who was gracious enough to take my call. I feel bad to this day that I put him through that.

The team stayed in the locker room for a long time, where there were very few dry eyes. As we said our goodbyes, I noticed Spike Owen over to the side. Had we won the College World Series that year, he probably would have been named MVP; his play was that great. Considering that, and the fact that he would be leaving us for the pros, made this pill much harder to swallow. Coach Gus would be quoted as saying, "Spike Owen is the best college shortstop I've ever seen." You'll find no arguments here.

It was a cruel hand I had dealt myself, and in the days that followed, I thought very privately as to how I was going to get over it. Losing this game in the manner in which it happened was nothing short of traumatic. I had dealt with setbacks before, but nothing like this. I was at a crossroads and knew that if I wanted to continue, I had better get over this and get my shit together. That would prove to be easier said than done, but I was determined to venture on and fight my way back. In my mind, it was the only way out and all I knew how to do.

· · ·

In the months that followed, I began to realize that the thoughts of that evening were consuming me. My father offered very little in terms of remedies or consolation, and Coach Gus offered nothing at all. At the age of nineteen, I was stranded on my own little island of misery, which had become a common theme in my life whenever I found myself in a crisis. I knew better than anyone that figuring a way off this island would be an undertaking that fell squarely on my shoulders. I began this journey by going back to Liberal, Kansas, where I completely sucked, leaving with a 6–5 record. The year before, summer ball was the place where I had found so much, and I really believed it would once again be the remedy for all I was facing, but I was wrong. By the time I made my way back to Austin, the sobering reality was that I was confused and dejected. There's no other way to describe it. I aimlessly stumbled forward in search of a solution whose very existence I began to doubt. It was a trying time for me and with fall practice looming; nothing looked good, and I was all out of answers.

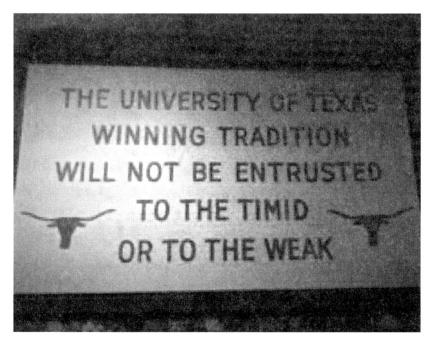

The unyielding message in our locker room. Coach Gus never let us forget it.

Playing for the Texas Longhorns was a dream come true but I had a lot to overcome going into my junior year.

Chapter 5

CHASING REDEMPTION

Don't be pushed around by the fears in your mind. Be led by the dreams in your heart. —ROY T. BENNETT

FALL PRACTICE in preparation for the 1983 season finally arrived, and I discovered that being around the guys again was therapeutic. I also was relieved to see that they were focused on the job at hand and didn't give a shit about what had happened the season before. Watching them grind it out each day with concentrated effort was truly inspiring and provided just the remedy I was looking for. Through their actions, I realized that they held nothing against me and, more importantly, were expecting me to contribute to the upcoming season. The message was loud and clear, and within only a few days of fall camp, I had escaped my lonely island and was back as a contributing member of the team. The negative thoughts were gone, and I was surrounded by a team who believed in me. I was back, and I couldn't have felt any better.

During the off-season, something wonderful happened which I hadn't noticed because my mental state had blinded me from almost everything. My weight returned almost out of nowhere, and I now carried 210 pounds on my 6′5″ frame. This was a big deal because, along with the added weight, my fastball returned—and it returned with a vengeance. For three years, the drastic weight loss which resulted from that strep-related illness had cost me my fastball. Given no choice and because I wanted to survive as a collegiate pitcher, I was forced to develop and master my curveball and slider. With my fastball reinstated, I had a deeper arsenal of pitches from which to choose, giving me an advantage in the ongoing chess match played between me and the guy with the bat. At this level, even the slightest edge can have a tremendous impact, and this positive turn of events proved to be a real game-changer for me.

Just like my fastball, spring also returned, bringing with it the start of the 1983 baseball season. Like all years, we had a number of new players who were introduced in the fall, but the one who really stood out was a well-built first baseman named Jose Tolentino. This kid was really good. The top pitchers, to no real surprise, came out of fall practice basically the same as they had the previous year. They were Killingsworth, Clemens, Capel, me, and (sprinkled into the mix) a crafty left-hander named Steve Labay. We began the season on everybody's radar and were ranked number one in the nation based largely on the number of accomplished pitchers we had returning.

As it would turn out, we didn't have to worry about breaking any winning streaks this year or even holding on to our top ranking because both vanished almost immediately. We started losing right away, falling to teams we had no business losing to. It was the most baffling thing you've ever seen. Capel and Clemens both lost at home to small NAIA schools, and what's worse, Clemens found himself at an unthinkable 0–2 early on. Mind you, this was the softest part of the schedule. It was so shocking that even Coach Gus was at a loss for words and spared us the nasty beat downs that were commonplace when such mediocrity was displayed. This is where Coach Gus deserves a lot of credit. He knew exactly how elite Clemens was, and he sounded no alarms, giving Roger the space necessary to work it out. And work it out, he did.

By the time conference play started, the Texas Longhorns were on a roll again with a 32–7 record, a regained number one ranking, and most importantly, Clemens and Capel were more dominant than they had ever been. I was having a terrific year and felt better on the mound than I ever had in my life. The fastball was my strongest weapon. As we entered Southwest Conference play, I was 5–0 with an ERA of 1.26. Our fielding and bats were once again exceptional. My classmate, Mike Brumley, had the formidable task of replacing Spike Owen at shortstop and was doing a fantastic job. Jose Tolentino was everything advertised and was smashing the cover off the ball at every opportunity. Unlike the year before, when we flew out of the gate firing on all cylinders, this team started slowly but improved with each and every outing. We marched purposefully towards our first meaningful goal—to win the Southwest Conference.

Cruising through the SWC schedule, Coach Gus put me on the mound against a tough TCU team. In my previous outing, I had thrown a three-hit shutout against Arkansas and was really in a groove. On this particular night against the Horned Frogs, I felt I had put it all together. Everything in my arsenal was working, and I was mowing batters down left and right, despite a blustery wind blowing in my face all night. As we headed into the last inning, I had a no-hitter going. I struck out the first two batters and was one out away from potentially securing it. The next batter hit a really high fly ball which appeared innocent, and heading for an easy out.

Unfortunately, the wind got a hold of it and took it further and further back until it finally landed hopelessly just on the other side of the outfield fence. I lost the no-hitter on a windblown home run. Even worse, we lost the game. No, I wasn't devastated or discouraged—I was absolutely livid! Yes, I'm both aware of and impressed by the fact that the opposing pitcher was throwing a gem of his own. After all, we hadn't scored either, but his wasn't a no-hitter given up the way this one was. Sometimes, the game of baseball has its own way of keeping you honest, but you have to do what I did and just move on, albeit with a little red ass in tow.

We went on to win the conference championship, and I finished with an 8–1 record, 1.89 ERA, and was named SWC Pitcher of the Year by the conference coaches. The team marched full stride toward the ever-important Southwest Conference Tournament, where the victor's prize was a home-field advantage as host of the NCAA Regional Tournament.

I opened up against Rice University and threw a seven strikeout, five-hit complete game for a 4–3 win. Mike Capel pitched a beauty the next night as we defeated Arkansas, 9–2. We were now in the finals, awaiting the winner of the loser's bracket, and regardless of opponent, they'd have to beat us twice. It was Arkansas, and we had Clemens on the mound. He pitched a good game, but we lost 5–4. The loss was discouraging for Roger because he had the Razorbacks off-balance all night. The good news was that in the first three games, our pitching staff had only given up a total of fourteen hits. All statistics aside, we now faced a second and final game against Arkansas. Coach Gus gave me the nod, and I threw a five-hit, complete-game shutout. Our bats sang all night long as we cruised to a 14–0 victory. The Longhorns secured the Southwest Conference title, Jose Tolentino was named tournament MVP, the NCAA Regionals were headed home to Austin, and we had met our first postseason goal.

As I mentioned earlier, the NCAA Regional Tournament was a big deal for our city. We had a loyal and ever-growing fan base, and having the opportunity to once again play in front of them was a distinct advantage for us. We were the number one ranked team in America, and our burnt orange-wearing, Hook 'em Horns-flashing fans couldn't have been prouder. We opened up against Northwest Louisiana with Clemens on the mound. He was brilliant, pitching a complete game shutout to advance us to Round 2 against Mississippi State. I was given the reins for this one, and it didn't go well. I walked eight batters, gave up six hits, and we lost to the Bulldogs, 6–2. We were sent to the loser's bracket, where we had to win three games in a row to advance. Keep in mind, unlike the conference tournament, where you could advance even if you didn't win, you had to win Regionals in order to receive an invitation to the College World Series. This meant that one more loss and our season was over. Our quest for three consecutive wins began with Pan American University, and Killingsworth threw a nice, four-hit complete game supported by outstanding hitting to secure an 11–3 win.

Now the stage was set, and we would have to beat Mississippi State twice to move on. Steve Labay, our crafty left-hander, was given the start and proved he deserved it by throwing a desperately needed, complete-game shutout—Longhorns 7, Bulldogs 0. We had battled all the way back, and now it was down to the final game, winner takes all, with "all" in this case being a trip to Omaha. Coach Gus couldn't afford to leave anything on the table and started Roger Clemens, with me waiting in relief. Roger was superb, throwing seven strong innings before Gus handed it over to me. I closed the Bulldogs out in the ninth, striking out the final batter in front of 7,000 grateful and rabid fans—a sea of burnt orange. The celebration in Austin was on. It was a 12–3, tag teamed, thumping buttressed by some damned impressive hitting along the way. Coach Gus openly admired our resilience, and his compliments flowed in a way I had never heard before. Although it was a side of him seldom seen and it was refreshing to finally witness. We were headed back to Omaha with one thing (and only one thing) on our minds: bringing the National Championship back to Austin.

These were special times for me. I was in complete control of my game, which for an athlete, is an incredibly cool thing to experience. What's more, The Associated Press had awarded me First Team All-American honors, while *Baseball America Magazine* named me "the best pitcher in college baseball." It was all very special, but I felt no added pressure from the accolades. In fact, if anything, they further boosted my confidence because they acknowledged that I was playing at a very high level.

All things considered, I was a year older, a year wiser, had traveled through hell and back, and was finally reunited with my fastball.

Deep in my heart, I embraced everything about returning to Omaha, the place that had damaged me so severely the year before. One of the sad truths of life is that the opportunity for redemption is rarely granted. I was lucky, blessed, and grateful for this chance, and I also knew I had done my part in preparing for an unlikely event whose day may have never come. When we boarded the plane for Omaha, the reality of this improbable scenario set in, and I give you my word when I say that fear, reluctance, and anxiety did not accompany me on this trip.

In our first game of the 1983 College World Series, Coach Gus put me on the mound for our matchup against James Madison University. We came out hot and never let up, pounding out sixteen hits and scoring twelve runs. I pitched a complete game, five-hit shutout for a 12–0 victory and a ticket to Round 2.

Next up were Oklahoma State Cowboys, a team consistently ranked among the best in college baseball. Although we clearly had their number the previous few seasons, they were never easy and always dangerous. Clemens got the call and was really good, striking out the first six batters and eleven altogether. It was a back and forth game marred by rare (but costly) errors by us. The game went into extra innings, where Killingsworth finished it off in the eleventh for a 6–5 victory. A theme had developed for our team in that we knew how to win close games. No matter how desperate the situation, we found a way to get it done, and gut-wrenching experiences in both the conference tournament and regionals had further strengthened our resolve. In the third round, we squared off against the University of Alabama and their superstar first baseman, Dave Magadan, named by *Baseball America Magazine* as the best hitter in all of college baseball.

Baseball is the ultimate team sport, so it's unusual to designate one individual (not a pitcher) who can consistently change the outcome of a game. Magadan was one of these rare athletes, and at 6'3", this left-handed first baseman lit up college baseball in 1983 and posted numbers unimaginable today. He finished the regular season with an unheard-of .525 batting average, and two games into the

Series held a jaw-dropping .882. Coach Gus knew that controlling this guy would be vital for us, and being that he was a left-handed batter, he decided to start our lefty pitcher, Steve Labay. It's a long-held belief in baseball that left-handed pitchers present left-handed hitters with a greater challenge due to the direction the ball breaks, as well as the fact that most batters don't have much experience facing lefties. Whatever the theory, that was Gus' strategy.

We scored on the Crimson Tide early and carried a 2–0 lead all the way into the fifth. Labay did an excellent job against Magadan, grounding him out twice and intentionally walking him once, so Coach's strategy was paying off. However, in the fifth, Alabama heated up, scored three runs, and put themselves into position to score even more. With two outs and runners in scoring position, Coach Gus pulled Labay, and in an attempt to quell their momentum, put me in. I retired the only batter I faced to get us out of the fifth, but we were now down, 3–2. We scored two runs in the top of the sixth to reclaim the lead, 4–3. I felt great and was throwing my fastball harder than ever. I retired the next six batters (which made seven in a row) to get us through the sixth and seventh innings. We were held scoreless during this stretch as well, and I entered the bottom half of the eighth with a 4–3 lead. The first batter I would face was none other than Dave Magadan. The much-anticipated matchup between two-All Americans was a showdown the 14,000 fans inside Rosenblatt Stadium had been waiting to see all night. The atmosphere was electric. *Baseball America's* best hitter facing off against *Baseball America's* best pitcher, and everybody watching understood the moment. I'd like to tell you that he was just another batter to me or that I didn't notice him at all, but that wouldn't be true. This dude was the best hitter college baseball had seen in a generation. I knew exactly who was at the plate.

It was going to be a fierce challenge, a high-stakes chess match of sorts, and I relished the opportunity to take him on. My first pitch was a ball. Another one followed, and I was immediately down in the count, 2–0. Needless to say, this was not an ideal situation. With my third pitch, I hung a slider—an ill-advised throw against a monster like Magadan, and he smashed that ball to the opposite field where it left the park for a solo home run. Rosenblatt stadium went absolutely crazy. Just like that, our chess match was over, and the game was tied, 4–4. As I stood on the mound, with a front-row seat watching Dave stroll around the bases, the intensity in the air was consuming—and it was about to get worse. The very next batter ripped me as well, driving a shot to the wall for a stand-up double. I now had a runner on second base with no outs. This is baseball, and this kind of shit happens, so you either bear down and keep grinding, or you get your ass handed to you in front of 14,000 fans and a nationally televised audience of millions. Those are the choices. At this stage in my career, I had the experience and mental toughness to avoid being rattled by the inevitable setbacks that occur during the course of a game. With that said, getting the next batter out was the only thought going through my head. I soldiered on and struck out the next three batters in succession, leaving a runner stranded on second. Until Magadan, I hadn't given up a run in twenty-one consecutive innings, and although it stung like hell, by the time I sat down in the dugout, I was over it.

We moved on to the ninth inning, where they held us scoreless, leaving the game tied 4–4. As I walked to the mound for the bottom half of the ninth, there was no way to ignore the electric atmosphere that was now defining this baseball game. I think it was obvious to everyone present that these were the best two teams in the tournament, and the winner of this game was likely to take it all the way. I quickly retired the first two batters, leaving us one out away from escaping the inning. The next batter up crushed my fastball for a double, and just like that, the winning run was at second base. I walked the next batter, which gave Bama runners on first and second with two outs. Next up (you guessed it) was Dave Magadan. As he strolled calmly to the batter's box, I saw something out of the corner of my eye which, at first, I tried to ignore, but for obvious reasons, couldn't. Coach Gus had left the dugout and was headed my way. He rarely came to the mound for any reason other than to change pitchers, so I knew what his intentions were. I wanted no part of it. As he approached the mound, and before he could say a word, I looked at him and said, "Don't do it, Coach. Don't take me out of this game." I'm not sure if he saw something in my eyes or what the hell happened; all I know is that he quietly nodded his head, told me to pitch him inside, and walked back to the dugout. The table for Round 2 was officially set. The situation we faced was as simple as it was extreme. Magadan needed a base hit to end the game, and I needed to get him out in order for us to stay alive and send this thing into extra innings. It was the ultimate showdown, in front of the ultimate fans taking place in the ultimate arena.

My first pitch was a strike, followed next by a foul ball. I had him down 0–2 in the count, and this time I was in control. My catcher Jeff Herron flashed me signs until we agreed on the next pitch and the electricity in the stadium kept us all aware of the situation at hand. I'm not exaggerating when I say that the next pitch I threw was the single hardest pitch I had ever thrown in my career. It was an inside fastball at which Magadan attacked with a huge swing and missed. Strikeout! The Rosenblatt crowd went completely nuts again and the game headed to extra innings. In the top of the tenth, our bats came alive, and we scored two runs to take a 6–4 lead. The tables had completely turned, and now Alabama would have to fight themselves off the ropes as we went in for the knockout. I went to the mound knowing that I was throwing harder and with more control than I ever had and was very confident that I was going to close them out. The bottom of the tenth didn't last long—three up, three down, and I had struck out every one of them to win the game. Of the sixteen batters faced, I struck out eleven and couldn't have been prouder. Steve Labay's stellar pitching took us to the middle innings, and as always, our hitters came through in the clutch. At the post-game news conference, I saw Dave Magadan in the distance. He saw me as well, and we nodded toward each other in a gesture of mutual respect. The two of us had faced off while at the top of our games, under the most extreme circumstances, and both landed decisive blows. What's more, we did it in front of the most deserving crowd in college baseball. It doesn't get better than that.

Our next game was against Michigan, who had the best team batting average in the tournament. Mike Capel pitched this one, and it was spectacular, perhaps the best of the tournament. He held the Wolverines to just four hits, and assisted by Mike Brumley's grand slam, secured a 4–2 victory. The Texas Longhorns were now the only undefeated team remaining. Alabama and Magadan fought their way through the loser's bracket, so now we would meet again for the National Championship. If we won, it was all over—we were the champs. But because we were undefeated, Alabama would have to beat us twice to win the title.

Coach Gus decided to pitch Clemens in the first game, and if a second game was needed, I would get the start. It wouldn't be necessary, though. Down 2–0 early, we came back and won the game 4–3. As usual, Magadan was superb, but Roger was even better and closed the deal as he had done so many times before. We were the National Champions of college baseball! The celebration on the mound was euphoric as the collection of guys Coach Gus had assembled finally got to let it all out and enjoy a once-in-a-lifetime experience as the undisputed kings of college baseball. The Rosenblatt Stadium crowd celebrated right along with us because they knew they had just witnessed something undeniably special and eagerly showed their appreciation. On the field, during the post-game ceremony, an NCAA official presented Coach Cliff Gustafson with the coveted National Championship Trophy. The team, along with our multitude of fans, exploded in cheers. The trophy was passed around, and when it got to me, I held it high in the air. The feeling was so powerful that it surpassed anything I had ever known. In that moment, it was as if the weight of the world had been lifted from my shoulders. I had found redemption. Then, as if designed by the moment itself, a voice came over the loudspeaker saying, "Calvin Schiraldi from The University of Texas has been named the Most Valuable Player of the 1983 College World Series."

What a difference a year had made.

Winning a National Championship is as rare as it gets. So many things have to be in place in order to reach such a pedestal. The 1983

Texas Longhorns had it all. Our hitters were exceptional, and our fielding was stellar. The pitching staff was deep and talented. The top four throwers on that staff (Killingsworth, Capel, Clemens, and myself) all won at least twelve games in 1983, and that feat remains unmatched in the history of Division 1 baseball.

And let's not forget the man who made it all possible. Coach Gus was a true legend who forged us all to be better versions of ourselves. He made it clear that mediocrity was a scourge and that it would be stamped out if it got anywhere near his baseball team. More importantly, he taught us that mastery can be achieved if you are willing to make the sacrifice necessary. To play for such a man and on the team he built was an experience like no other. I've grown to appreciate just how special it was.

Reflecting on my experiences at the College World Series, a number of things come to mind. As you know by now, I have an undying admiration for those who have the guts to enter the Arena, and I feel a special connection to them all. With that in mind, there is one person worthy of mention who epitomizes this warrior's spirit. After being struck in the face by my errant pitch the year before, Kevin Penner underwent multiple surgeries to repair his broken socket and damaged left eye. He experienced double vision so severe that doctors were unsure if it would ever go away. Kevin never gave up. He kept pushing forward, and when his physical wounds healed and the double vision subsided, he courageously set out to play baseball again. The fact that he had the courage to step back in the batter's box is inspiring enough, but Kevin went a step further. Equipped with a specially designed face shield, he returned to Wichita State, where he led the team with a .435 batting average, was named All-American, and drafted by the Texas Rangers. If the burning desire to win was ever on display, you'd find it inside Kevin Penner—a true badass.

• • •

As my time at The University of Texas came to an end, the next phase of my life was just beginning and looking brighter than I could have ever imagined. I finished my college career with a 29-6 record and was chosen in the first round by the New York Mets with the twenty-seventh pick of the 1983 Major League Draft. Many years later, I was inducted into The University of Texas Hall of Fame, which is one of the great honors of my life. I had grown considerably while on the Forty Acres, and the years there were much more than a collection of fond memories. I was part of a team that achieved success seldom seen or experienced by anyone at any level.

I endured lows so overwhelming that I questioned the existence of a way out. I discovered that navigating my way through these trials made me mentally stronger and provided the wisdom to recognize that if you dig deep enough, you can indeed recover from almost anything. I left college a different person—smarter, tougher, and decidedly more resilient than the young kid who came in. In the simplest of terms, I had become a man, and it was time to take what I had learned and move on to professional baseball. My experience at The University of Texas changed my life forever, and for the rest of my days, I will carry with me the knowledge and skills I developed there.

Hook 'em Horns.

Celebrating the win over Alabama at the College World Series after striking out the side in the tenth inning.

Austin American Statesman

Holding the coveted National Championship trophy. Roger and Coach Gus to my right.

Coach Cliff Gustafson, a true legend.

Capel, Clemens, Killingsworth, and me. All four winning at least twelve games in 1983. Still an NCAA record for a pitching staff.

The magical beacon. What an honor to be part of the team that lit it No. 1.

Chapter 6

THE GAUNTLET

A ship is safe in harbor, but that's not what ships are built for.
—JOHN G. SHEDD

THE NATIONAL CHAMPIONSHIP CELEBRATIONS were incredible. To honor our baseball team, The University of Texas lit its famed twenty-nine-story tower in burnt orange, highlighted with a massive (bright white) "No. 1" down the middle of it. This glorious beacon illuminated the night sky, as our city, in full celebration, welcomed home their National Champions with more fanfare than you could ever dream of. The scene around campus was nuts, people honking their horns, parties everywhere, and it lasted deep into the night. It was an amazing experience, to be sure—and one that I wished could have lasted forever—but unfortunately for me, it didn't last long at all.

Just ten short days after kissing the trophy at Rosenblatt Stadium, I was back at the bottom of the pecking order, having to prove myself all over again. I found myself in a town I had never heard of, playing on a team I didn't know and living in a crappy apartment with two complete strangers. Granted, I had $75,000 in my bank account for signing with the Mets, but other than that, I was just one of thousands of like-minded baseball players who were trying to make their way through the gauntlet—otherwise known as the Major League Baseball farm system. I was afforded no time to celebrate, no time to relax, no time to decompress, and no time to reflect. I had entered the world of professional baseball, and it was surreal. Virtually overnight, as if they never happened, the All-American and College World Series MVP titles had faded into darkness, and I was faced with the harsh reality that nobody at this level gave a shit about any of it. I was back at square one.

I arrived in Jackson, Mississippi, in June 1983, where I was assigned to a Class AA (more commonly known as Double-A) minor league team. I immediately entered the rotation but was mentally exhausted with a right arm spent from having pitched 140 innings over the previous five months. These were interesting (and challenging) times to say the least. Despite the whirlwind engulfing me, the situation was markedly different than in the past. When Coach Gus threatened to take away my scholarship in '81, I was truly lost and sincerely questioned whether or not I had what it took to compete at the collegiate level. This was not the case when I arrived in Jackson. I had a singular focus to reach the majors, compete, and win at baseball's highest level. My focus never wavered from this objective, and I was confident that I had the mental and physical ability to get there. All of my experiences, from childhood to Westlake and then Texas, had prepared me for this particular time and place, and I was hell-bent on taking what I'd learned and going after what I wanted. To my mind, it was just a matter of time.

My goals and confidence were certainly real, but some might argue, a bit naïve. Think of the Major League farm system as a kind of pyramid, where the top represents the big leagues or, as players call it, "The Show." At the bottom of the pyramid is the Rookie League, followed in succession by Single-A, Double-A, Triple-A, and finally, the Majors. I referred to this earlier as a gauntlet because there really is no other way to adequately describe it. When you consider that only a small percentage of little leaguers are good enough to play in high school and even a smaller number of high schoolers are good enough to play in college, and of that group, only a tiny fraction get drafted, by the time you get to the professional baseball, you're dealing with the best players on the planet. If that isn't daunting enough, consider that there are thousands of these guys who have made it to this level and are giving everything they have to make it all the way. The grinding competition created by this mass of talent greets you on day one. And if that's still not daunting enough, with every step up the pyramid, you're exposed to even greater competition and an even more refined skill level. Considering this, it's no wonder that less than one percent of all baseball players ever make it to the top. This is the gauntlet, and in the summer of 1983, it was my new world. Getting through it would be the greatest challenge I had ever faced.

Being assigned to the Double-A Jackson Mets meant I had skipped over all of the guys in Rookie ball and Single-A before ever throwing a single professional pitch. Although baseball is business in its purest form and my placement was simply a business move, there was still a feeling among players that starting out in Double-A meant you hadn't paid the proper dues expected of an MLB system participant. My new teammates were older than me, and almost everyone one of them had gone through the first two stages of the gauntlet, with some taking years to do it. Needless to say, from the outset, I felt pressure to prove I belonged and sought to earn the respect of players who perceived me as one who cut in line. This was a different type of pressure altogether, and like so many other obstacles I had faced, I'd have to figure out how to get through this one too.

Jackson was a quiet little town offering Southern hospitality and fans who loved their baseball team. I fell in love with it immediately. Roger McDowell, a talented Jackson pitching prospect, was kind enough to show me around. For the first week, the Mets put me up in a hotel. They also provided a monthly salary of $750, which was supposed to cover all of my living expenses. Even back in 1983, $750 was not all that much, so it was a struggle to make ends meet. After that first week, I was responsible for making my own living arrangements, which traditionally meant finding teammates willing to take you in. Kevin Mitchell and Herm Winningham had an apartment with room for one more, so I became their roommate. As I said, everyone at this level was really good, and Herm and Kevin were no exception. Both of these guys eventually made it to the top and enjoyed accomplished major league careers. Regardless of all that, I was relieved to have my housing situation settled with good roommates. The stability enabled me to concentrate on the task at hand.

For me, life in the pros, especially at this level, was not all fun and games like you might expect it to be. As I mentioned before, I'm not an outgoing person, so I wasn't hitting the town every night or living the pro-athlete lifestyle so often portrayed in the media. Minor league ball was a grind. From the countless number of games to the brutal travel schedule and never-ending bus rides, there wasn't much time for anything else. Try to imagine this. The season lasts from April through August, and during this 150-day period, there were 140 games scheduled. That means you're playing games almost non-stop. If the game began at 7:00pm, you were to be at the field before 4:00pm, and you wouldn't arrive home until close to midnight—and that's only if the game is at home. Road games were far more demanding because we traveled to Tulsa, El Paso, Midland, San Antonio, Little Rock, and Beaumont almost exclusively by bus. That took some getting used to, and for athletes who were always expected to be at their best, it was a challenge, to say the least.

Shortly after my arrival, I was put into the rotation with very mixed results. The talent I was facing in Double-A ball was similar to that at the elite college level, so being caught off guard was not the problem. In other words, the talent gap I had experienced coming from high school into the University of Texas was far greater than that between UT and Double-A. The only discernible difference was that in college, you could always find a weakness, but here, weaknesses of any kind were scarce. I was 2–3 after my first five games with a 5.82 ERA which was obviously high. By now, I had been playing in Jackson for nearly six weeks, and we were traveling to Beaumont, where I was slated to start. I won that game, moving my record to 3–3, and when we arrived back in Jackson, I got called into the office. Having no idea what to expect, good or bad, the coach told me that upper management had decided to move me down to Single-A and that I was to report to Lynchburg, Virginia, the very next day. Just like that, the gauntlet had kicked my ass down the pyramid and out of Jackson, Mississippi, as if to say, "Welcome to the world of professional baseball, Mr. Schiraldi."

As it turned out, being sent down to Lynchburg was not much of a demotion after all. Granted, it was a Single-A team, but that year, the Lynchburg Mets had the best record of any team in the entire system. They were loaded with impressive young players headlined by outfielders Mark Carreon and Lenny Dykstra, catcher Greg Olsen, and a pitcher named Dwight Gooden. Another advantage of being on this team was their youth. They were all younger than the Jackson players, and being around guys my own age made me much more comfortable. Lynchburg became my home for the next five weeks, and the experience was time well spent.

A new town and new team allowed me to catch my breath and relax a little. I don't mean "relax" like going to the beach, but more in terms of my surroundings. Like Jackson, I was plugged into the rotation right away and achieved better results from the start. I almost doubled the number of strikeouts in my time there, despite the fact that I threw eight less innings than in Jackson. As a team, we were outstanding, cruising through the playoffs and ultimately being crowned Champions of the Carolina League, which is as far as a team could go. Imagine being on two significant championship teams within three months of each other. It was pretty cool, to say the least.

That season, the Lynchburg Mets won ninety-nine games, which was the most of any team in all of pro baseball. Although I had only joined them for the last five weeks, the experience was really good for me. I finished my time in Lynchburg with a 4–1 record and a 4.45 ERA. More importantly, I gained vital knowledge of the system and the players within it, and that would prove extremely valuable as I headed into my second year. After the season ended, I went back home to Austin for some much-needed rest.

There's no way to properly describe the mental, emotional, and physical whirlwind I experienced in the first nine months of 1983. I was on a team that won the Collegiate National Championship, drafted into the major leagues, spent three grueling months inside the gauntlet, and capped it off as a member of the Single-A championship team. By the time I arrived back in Austin in mid-September, I was numb with exhaustion. During the previous seven months, I had thrown 208 innings of competitive baseball, and it had taken a serious toll on my body and my mind. For the next five months, my only objective was to rest and get completely away from baseball. I fully committed to decompressing and recall this time as being free of stress and among the most enjoyable periods of my life.

We often hear people say that they feel like they have a new lease on life, and by the time February rolled around, it's precisely how I felt. The time off was rejuvenating, as it allowed me to relax among family and close friends. Best of all, I was invited to participate in the annual UT alumni baseball game.

The University of Texas has a wonderful tradition of hosting a game pitting Texas alums, now in the pros, against the current team. The game opens up the new season for the program, and the Longhorn faithful love it. Returning to campus and reuniting with Spike, Roger, Steve, Mike, and the rest of the guys was special for me, and the event was a whole lot of fun. As an added bonus, Coach Gustafson greeted me and smiled from ear to ear when we embraced. I saw him laugh and cut up with his former players as if we were long-lost high school buddies. The pride that gleamed in his eyes while surrounded by his professional alums was a sight to behold, and I'll never forget it. This staunch disciplinarian showed a fun-loving side that we Texas Exes were never allowed to see while under his leadership. As a Longhorn player, I didn't always like the way Gus did things, but there's no denying the profound impact this man had on my life. Having the opportunity to interact with him in this way brought our relationship full circle, and I have enjoyed being in his presence ever since. With all that said, the alumni event was awesome and the perfect way to end my offseason. By the way, and in case you're wondering, we beat the shit out of those young college kids.

In March 1984, I reported to spring training in Florida after spending five full months away from the game. My body hadn't felt this good in years, and my mind was refreshed and clear. The time off was crucial and something that, in the past, I had never been afforded. In high school, I was always running from one sport to the next, and in college, baseball was a year-round venture. Throw school work on top of all of that, and there simply wasn't time to get the proper rest my body and mind needed. In terms of rest, no period demanded it more than 1983. I spoke earlier of the staggering number of innings I pitched during this time, as well as the amount of game travel required. At the time, I didn't realize just how worn down I was. After the break ended and I arrived back at spring practice, I finally appreciated how good my body felt. It was a game-changer for me, and the benefits of rest became noticeable right away.

I had a good spring camp, and in recognition of my performance, I was once again assigned to the Double-A Jackson Mets. Not only was this a good sign, but the situation was also vastly improved because I was starting at the same time as everyone else and playing in a familiar place. Best of all, the team was almost entirely made up of players from the same Lynchburg team for whom I'd pitched the year before. I rented a house, which was more comfortable than an apartment, with Billy Beane, Dwayne Vaughn, and Ed Hearne (all great guys) as my roommates. The minor league scene was no longer a maze of confusion and uncertainty, and I felt a genuine sense of calm as the season began.

Although my early record of 1–2 might not indicate it, I was pitching extremely well to start the 1984 season. My ERA was 1.21, and I had complete control of my game. As April turned into May, the wins began to pile up, and I found myself with a 7–2 record. The team was also winning, and although the season was still young, it became apparent that the Jackson Mets were the team to beat in Double-A.

I would love to say that the team was gelling or the team was coming together as a group, but in this environment, the whole concept of team is likely different from anything you've ever experienced before. I realized from day one that true teams, like those I had played for in high school and college, didn't exist here. The gauntlet doesn't allow it. I'm in no way suggesting that the players don't get along or that managers are discounted. I'm just saying that the success of the team is completely secondary to the development and success of the individual. In other words, upper management doesn't give a shit whether a minor league team wins or loses a championship, just as long as they are producing players that can help them win at the highest level. It's just the way it is, and it didn't mean that we, as players, didn't enjoy each other or play well together. It just meant that the whole concept of team was secondary to everything else, and that makes the approach to the game different and much more individualized. With that said, the Jackson Mets were really good.

We weren't allowed too many days off, but I remember that during one of them, sometime in the middle of May, I was relaxing on the couch when a young woman from Jackson, who was dating one of my roommates, stopped by to visit. Nothing unusual there, except this time she brought along a friend. This was the first time I laid eyes on Debbie Murphy. She was beautiful and carried herself with both confidence and grace, which made me wonder, "What the hell is she doing over here?" We struck up a conversation, and I was immediately drawn to her sense of humor. I also was equally impressed with how genuine she was. Best of all her personality had an edge to it and I loved that. I wasn't a seasoned professional in this particular arena (not even close), but I knew I had to find a way to go out with her.

Somehow, someway, she agreed, and when my schedule allowed, we went on a few dates. Deb was a junior at Mississippi State, and it just so happened that her Bulldogs were playing my Longhorns in the college baseball playoffs, so we watched the game together, ribbing each other the entire time. The evening couldn't have gone better. These were special times, and being around Deb was quickly becoming the highlight of my week.

As anyone who has ever played baseball can tell you, sometimes you just get on a roll. I was on such a roll heading into June and was throwing better than ever. Around this time, it was announced I had made the Double-A All-Star Team, which was quite an honor. Not only that, I was chosen as the starter. What really made this recognition special was that it was verification from outside the Mets organization that I was accomplishing things at this level. The All-Star game was played in Jackson, and I remember how much fun it was— as well as the experience of being surrounded by so many talented players. The rest of June and all of July flew by, and I was still on a roll. My record going into August was 14–3 with a 2.88 ERA, and as the postseason approached, the Jackson Mets were on pace to break the record for most wins in team history. Little did I know, I wouldn't be chasing that record with them. On August 1, I was summoned to the coach's office and informed that upper management had assigned me to the Tidewater Tides, a Triple-A club in Norfolk, Virginia. My promotion was a big one and a giant step toward my goal of getting to the Big Leagues. The way I saw it, I would get introduced to Triple-A that year and, in 1985, would start out in Tidewater, where if I did well, by the end of next season I would have a real shot at making it to the Majors. Every aspect of my life seemed to be aligning, including my relationship with that beautiful girl from Jackson, which was growing stronger by the day.

I was reunited in Tidewater with my rookie-year roommates, Herm Winningham and Kevin Mitchell, and although I wasn't living with them, it was nice to be around familiar faces. Like before, I was immediately thrown into the rotation, and fortunately for me, picked up right where I left off in Jackson. I always respected the talent level I was facing in the pros, but by now, I was no longer intimidated by it. A mantra that I would always repeat to myself was, "Just relax and throw, just relax and throw." This was easier said than done when I first arrived in pro ball, but by the summer of 1984, I had figured out how to do it.

I was pitching better in Tidewater than I was in Jackson and would end up with a 3–1 record and a 1.09 ERA. I was at the top of my game and now sitting close to the top of the pyramid. I couldn't stop thinking that Tidewater in 1985 would be the perfect launching point for me to make a run at the Big Leagues and that next year could finally be my breakthrough. When I was called into the office at the end of August, I suspected two things would happen. One, management would confirm that I had a great season and that I was close, and two, I would get my marching orders and workout assignments for the offseason. Those were my expectations. What I didn't expect to hear was that I was being called up to New York and, in five days, would be pitching in Shea Stadium for the New York Mets. I left the office thinking, "Holy shit."

Despite having a good year in both Double-A and Triple-A, I never gave a single thought to the possibility of getting called up in 1984. I knew I had improved my chances for the 1985 season and thought I might have a shot then, but this chain of events completely blindsided me. I had a thousand thoughts swirling through my mind ranging from pure exhilaration to anxiety in its rawest form. To help settle the craziness of the situation, I asked Deb to drive with me to New York, and she agreed. Getting to know her over the past three months had been a godsend, and sharing this experience with her would further strengthen our already growing relationship.

I was never a big city guy and had no experience in dealing with that life, so you can imagine how I felt when I became completely lost in the middle of New York City, trying to find my way to Shea Stadium. To this day, I don't know what happened. I think I took the Lincoln Tunnel when I shouldn't have. Then, I went looking for the Brooklyn Bridge and drove around Manhattan in circles, trying to find it. It took three hours, and for the last part of it, I had my windows rolled down and was blaring Hank Williams music as high as my radio would allow. The whole scene was nuts. I finally reached the stadium, barely in time for my first meeting. That was my miserable introduction to New York, but for obvious reasons, it was soon forgotten.

Upon my arrival, I was shown around Shea Stadium, which was something to behold. With a capacity of 57,000, it was four times larger than any stadium I had ever pitched in. I remember walking around the facility in near disbelief that I, as a ballplayer, was actually there. When I entered the locker room, it hit me. There it was, my very own locker, and inside it hung a New York Mets jersey with with my name stitched on the back. I had officially made it through the gauntlet, and regardless of how long I'd be allowed to stay, this was one of the proudest moments of my life.

I spent my first game taking in the view with the relief pitchers inside the bullpen. There is no way to adequately describe the raucous atmosphere produced by the Mets fans at Shea. There is no other way to say it except that it was mind-blowing. My first taste of this came early in the game when, in the stands, an all-out fan brawl broke out between off-duty police officers and off-duty firefighters. You couldn't make this shit up if you tried. The game carried on during this melee, but everyone was watching the fight instead of the game, including most of the players. Fighting in the stands was commonplace, as was the throwing of beer and other projectiles. Also, of course, there was the merciless and never-ending taunting of opposing players. It was a complete zoo, and I had never in my life experienced anything close to it. Thankfully for me, these fans were fanatical about their Mets, which for the time being, afforded me protection from the madness.

The day finally arrived when I took the mound in the second game of a doubleheader against the San Diego Padres. I tried, but the fact was, it was damn near impossible for me to go out there and treat this game like any other. Don't even think about that "Relax and throw" shit because relaxing was no longer part of the equation. I'd been playing baseball since I was nine, and this moment was fulfilling a lifelong dream. I was in a New York Mets uniform at Shea Stadium pitching in front of 50,000 fans. It's hard to describe what was going through my head and to be perfectly honest, I'm not sure I even knew. Despite the fact that I was pitching better than I ever had going into this contest, I got my ass shelled and was out of the game by the third inning. What's worse, I was booed as I came off the field. This entire experience was surreal and went by in a flash. Results aside, I ended up taking more from this game than from almost any other because the exposure to this atmosphere was the key to understanding it, and understanding it was the key to managing it. It was just going to take time and more games to get comfortable, and I knew that I had taken the ever-important first step toward getting there.

When I left the stadium that evening, I understood that I was in the beginning stages of a long and difficult journey, and I knew at that moment that I didn't want to make it alone. Deb and I went out that evening, and I asked her to marry me. She said yes. Being with her brought me a real sense of joy at a time when I was living a very challenging and uncertain life. Our engagement and knowing that she would be by my side made this the most beautiful night of my life. Deb is that special to me.

Although I had arrived in New York toward the end of the season, I was still afforded a few more opportunities to play. My second start was against the Montreal Expos, which was better than my first outing, but not by much. That night, Dan Driessen hit a home run off me that went so far I'm not sure it ever landed. We lost that game, 5–2. My last appearance came in Chicago when they put me in for middle relief. I pitched well that day, and I remember Keith Hernandez approaching me after the game and saying, "Good job out there. We're going to need a middle reliever next year. Keep it up." I was beginning to feel more comfortable, and his words sure didn't hurt. Like I said, it's all about getting big-league exposure and big-league reps, and by the time the season ended, I had a good dose of both. What an amazing year it had been.

In the spring of 1985, I reported to my first Major League spring training camp in St. Petersburg, Florida. It was an incredible experience which probably would have been much more intimidating if not for my big league exposure at the close of '84. Most of the time at camp was spent scrimmaging against other teams in order to get innings in, which created stats and film for management to evaluate.

My most vivid memory from this camp was being surrounded daily by the who's who of Major League Baseball. Here I was, pitching against the likes of Pete Rose and Mike Schmidt and having to keep my shit together while doing it. By now, I was well aware that this wasn't an autograph show or a meeting of the mutual admiration society. It was all business, and I approached it as such, even though it was pretty cool competing against these guys. I had a very good camp, and it ultimately came down to a decision for one roster spot between Roger McDowell and me. Roger was the guy who showed me around Jackson when I first arrived in pro ball, so I, of course, knew him pretty well. He was an excellent pitcher and had been throwing some nasty stuff all spring. In the end, he won the position (deservedly so), which meant I was heading back to Triple-A Tidewater. Being called up in 1984, coupled with spring training the following year, were both incredibly important to my development. Pro baseball was no longer a maze of uncertainty. I now knew what the top of the pyramid looked and felt like and was confident I would get back there soon.

I spent the 1985 season alternating between Tidewater and New York. I was called up in April and got my first major league win against the St. Louis Cardinals. In May, I pitched against the Atlanta Braves and took a line drive off my left foot, which splintered the bone in my little toe. Even though it was just my little toe, it was painful as hell. For the next two months, I cut a hole in my cleat to accommodate the swelling and relieve the pain. What made things worse was that the injury was on my left foot, the one put under tremendous pressure with every throw. Worst of all and out of necessity, my mechanics changed, which was not a good thing in the middle of a Major League season. Regardless, by late August, my foot was feeling much better, and I finished the season on the Mets roster. I ended 1985 with ten Major League starts, a 2–1 record, and a very high ERA thanks in large part to a game against Philadelphia where I got hammered by the Phillies and gave up ten runs in less than two innings. Until the very end, the Mets were in the hunt for the pennant but would eventually fall to St. Louis, missing the playoffs.

I didn't have a great season by any stretch, but it wasn't a disaster either, and my understanding of playing at this level had grown immensely. For me, the initial whirlwind (and sometimes consuming environment) that can engulf a new Major League player became less of a factor, and I was feeling more relaxed within the setting. All things considered, 1985 had been crucial for my development, and I felt a real sense of confidence going into the offseason.

As for the Mets, the world was beginning to align perfectly. Their minor league teams had been terrorizing the league over the past few years, and now those young, talented players were ascending to the top. Everyone in baseball knew that it was only a matter of time before we would make the playoffs and perhaps even compete for a World Championship. One group knew this better than anyone—the notorious Mets fans who hadn't seen a championship in eighteen years. An undeniable fever engulfed the Big Apple, and the Mets players were well aware of it. We knew 1986 could be the year, and like the rest of my teammates, I was determined to be a part of it.

In November, surrounded by family and friends, Deb and I were married in her hometown of Jackson, Mississippi. Ours was a wonderful ceremony, and Deb was as beautiful a bride as I could have possibly imagined. I was so excited to begin my new life with her. Over the past years, I had traveled a long way and was now a totally different player and person than who I was coming in. I had found and married the girl of my dreams, and I had entered the world of professional baseball. On the career side, nothing could have prepared me for what I had gotten into. The gauntlet was real and everything that I described it to be. This system, albeit brutal and cutthroat, is designed to forge players into being the best they can be and discard the rest. Making it through this stage was a tremendous accomplishment, achieved by very few, which made me appreciate it even more. Understanding this, I couldn't help but think of my dad, Coach Bushong, Gus, and all of the wonderful teammates and coaches from my earlier years, because without them, I had no chance of making it this far. With that said, getting through the gauntlet was not my goal. My goal was always to compete and win at the highest level baseball could offer, and I had yet to do that. My performance in the minors had been a success, but my performance in the big leagues, to this point, was subpar and I, more than anyone, understood this. My focus moving forward was to win, nothing more and nothing less.

• • •

One week after our wedding, while we were still on our honeymoon, I received word that the Mets had traded me to the Boston Red Sox. The news came out of nowhere, and I have to admit, it was a little shocking. I had spent the past three years getting comfortable with my surroundings, and just like that, I was sent packing from the only place I knew. Here was the business side of baseball, and if the gauntlet had taught me anything, it was that comfort would seldom if ever, be a part of the journey. It took a few days to process, but the more I thought about it, the more excited I became about going to Boston. It was going to be a great opportunity for me, and besides, Roger Clemens was there, and our wives were friends, so it wasn't like Deb and I wouldn't know anyone. The way I saw it, being on a new team would be a great way to establish myself as a successful pitcher in the Majors, and since that had always been my goal, Boston would be the perfect place to achieve it. It all made sense to me, and I set my sights on 1986, determined and excited to make it happen with the Red Sox.

Me with the Jackson Mets. The gauntlet was very real and I knew
that I wasn't at Texas anymore

That beautiful girl from Jackson (Debbie Murphy), who would become my wife.

Chapter 7

BOSTON

We must dare, and dare again, and go on daring.
—George Jacques Danton

AT THE START of the 1986 season, I was twenty-three years old and had been pitching competitively for well over a decade—including two and a half years in the pros. I'd learned a lot during this time. The arena where a pitcher competes is different from almost any other in sports. Granted, baseball is a team sport, but there's a game—highly individualized and integral to every outcome—being played within the game. I'm referring to the contest between pitcher and the batter, and in baseball, it's where the rubber meets the road. The dynamics of this battle are every bit mental as they are physical. It's competition in its purest form, matching equally determined individuals seeking a desired outcome at the other's expense. I loved everything about it.

There's a famous saying in baseball that suggests, "Good pitching beats good hitting and vice versa." As silly as this sounds, it's basically true. "Good" describes the outcome. If the batter gets on base, the batter wins. If the pitcher gets him out, the pitcher wins.

There are also thousands of variables that can impact the outcome, making each at-bat unique. For instance, the umpire can call a ball when the pitch was clearly a strike, giving the batter an advantage. By the same token, the umpire can call a pitch (that was clearly a ball) a strike, handing the pitcher the advantage. Coping with human errors, sometimes perceived and sometimes real, is a battle in and of itself because both the batter and the pitcher, if they hope to succeed, must be mentally tough enough to deal with them. Then you have the scenario where the batter crushes the ball, but the defense makes an incredible play and gets him out. In that instance, the pitcher wins, of course.

On the flip side, the pitcher causes the batter to pop up, the outfielder loses the easy out in the sun and drops it, and the batter wins. A routine ground ball takes a nasty hop and bounces over the shortstop's head. Batter wins. Or the batter smashes two straight pitches that barely go foul and then swings and misses on the third pitch. Pitcher wins. No matter how illogical it may seem, this is how it is. Sometimes, you throw your best pitch, and the batter takes it out of the yard, while the next time, you throw a crappy pitch, and the batter swings and misses for a strikeout. Finally, there is the variable of navigating the external environment, which could include the weather or tens of thousands of fans screaming for your demise at a time when the situation in the game itself is bearing down on you as well. During this turmoil, the batter has to find a way to hit a 90-plus mph baseball while the pitcher has to prevent a talented hitter from doing so. This high-stakes chess match is the ultimate arena, and ever since I was a kid, I've relished the opportunity to play in it.

From mid-February to the end of March, the Boston Red Sox held their spring training in Winter Haven, Florida. I was part of an eight-player trade which sent me, Wes Garner, John Christenson, and LaSchelle Tarver to Boston in exchange for John Mitchell, Bob Ojeda, Chris Bayer, and Tom McCarthy. The most talked-about aspect of the trade concerned Bob Ojeda and me. The issue was whether or not it was a good idea for Boston to trade an established major league starter in Ojeda for one of the top pitching prospects in the Mets organization, which happened to be me. I felt enormous pressure going into spring ball trying to prove that Boston didn't make a mistake, and almost immediately, the situation went south. In addition to battling the pressure of the trade, I was also forced to contend with tendonitis in my pitching arm. Since both lasted the duration of spring training, it didn't go well.

The next six weeks would be miserable, and I absolutely sucked. I was getting shelled in almost every outing which was not only humiliating and embarrassing, it put my career in jeopardy. At this level, one thing is for certain; you don't ever make the mistake of blaming something like tendonitis because excuses of any kind will only bring further disdain upon you. To this day, I can't say for sure what caused this crash. All I know is that it wasn't good, and no one gave a shit as to why. What they did care about was that Boston gave up a damn good pitcher for me, and a few weeks into spring ball, it appeared as if they really screwed up.

This marked the first time I had to face the truly ugly side of this profession. I hadn't been with Boston but for a few weeks, and already I was getting hammered by the media, as was the Red Sox front office. I felt worse about the heat the general manager was taking than any criticism toward me because it was my performance that was making him look bad. Up to this point in my career, I had faced almost every kind of pressure, but this was completely different and hard as hell for me to reconcile. There was only one viable way out of this situation, and it was to block everything out as best I could and start getting results. If I couldn't figure it out, it would spell the end of my career at age twenty-three.

For obvious reasons, I didn't make the Red Sox Roster and was sent down to start the season in the International League with our Triple-A team in Pawtucket, Rhode Island. At this point, I was pretty much at rock bottom, so being away from the spotlight would be a good thing for me as I began the process of clawing my way back. Initially, I didn't see much action in Pawtucket, which offered me no chance to work things out. However, as the season progressed, more and more pitchers were either being called up or moved around, and each time this happened, I would get additional opportunities to play. By May, my shoulder felt great, my mind was right, and I started to find my groove. I was beginning to establish myself as the team's top closer, and with every game, I got better and gained more confidence. Baseball is a crazy game. One moment nothing works, and you wonder if it will ever come back. The next moment, it's all clicking, and everything seems to go as planned. In the end, it's all about resilience. During this period, I remember feeling a genuine sense of relief because I had found my game again and fought my way back from the traumatic experience that was spring training. Although I was still in Triple-A, I knew that if I continued on this path, I had a real chance of being called up before the season ended.

By June, I was really on a roll and felt as good on the mound as I ever had. My new role was that of a closer, which was indeed different for me, but it was also something I became comfortable with. I always considered myself a starter, as I thought it best fit me, but in the business of baseball, you don't get to pick and choose where you want to be, and I was fine with that. Ironically, in an interview with a Boston newspaper, my old coach, Cliff Gustafson, was quoted as saying that he always thought I would be a closer in the major leagues and that it fit my mental and physical skill sets perfectly. Regardless of his thoughts or mine, I was a closer now and was both comfortable and excited about it.

We played my old team, the Tidewater Mets, a few times, and I pitched well each time I faced them. Again, it was still Triple-A, but succeeding against them worked wonders towards reducing the pressure of the trade. In fact, it went a long way in restoring my confidence. For the previous six weeks, I had been Pawtucket's top closer, and by the time July rolled around, I had pitched forty-four innings with sixty strikeouts and an ERA of 2.8. I was also leading the International League in saves with twelve. By this time, the stories about me in the media had begun to take a positive turn, but to be perfectly honest, I didn't give a shit. I had crossed that bridge, and nothing in the world mattered to me except being the best that I could be and getting back to the majors. Up to this point, I had done a good job of blocking everything out, and that was the only way to survive the situation I had gotten myself into.

As it turned out, I got my shot right after the All-Star break when Boston placed middle reliever Steve Crawford on injured reserve. The chance that I thought I had blown was back in front of me again, and this time my body was healthy, and I was pitching extremely well. The Red Sox were on a nine-day West Coast road trip when I was told to report immediately and join the team in Seattle. It had taken three months of facing grueling internal turmoil, but I had fought my way back to the Big Leagues. They say what doesn't kill you makes you stronger. In terms of my career, spring ball almost killed me, but in the end, it didn't, and true to the saying, I came out of it stronger than ever. For the first time since turning pro, I knew I belonged, and I knew what to expect. I was in a really good place and was looking forward to joining my new teammates as quickly as I could.

The prospects for the 1986 Boston Red Sox, at least according to the baseball writers, were not very good at all. The preseason predictions had us finishing a distant fourth in our division. By mid-season, these predictions were not holding up, and when I joined the team in July, the Red Sox were sitting on top of the division as one of the hottest teams in baseball. In all fairness to the writers, there were several factors they couldn't have predicted preseason. First and foremost, there was the dominance being displayed by Roger Clemens, who had come out of almost nowhere and completely dominated the major leagues. In April, he became the first player in history to strike out twenty batters in a single game. He was the hottest pitcher in baseball and was selected to play in the 1986 MLB All-Star Game, which he not only started but was also named MVP. Bruce Hurst and Dennis Ray "Oil Can" Boyd were also on the staff, with both throwing at an exceptionally high level. The hitting on this team was outstanding and would get even better after a few late-season trades. Needless to say, I was excited to be a part of it.

I met the team on the West Coast and got my first opportunity in Seattle. Our coach, who had been around the league a long time, was John McNamara. I didn't know much about Mac, but he was a nice guy with a relaxed demeanor who let you do your thing. My role was as a middle reliever or "inning eater" as they were known back then. A middle reliever enters the game during the early innings to relieve the starter. The expectations are that you get through the middle innings and hopefully go deep enough so that the closer can take over. In other words, you're eating innings and saving the arms of the rest of the pitching staff.

We were losing to Seattle in the third when I was put in for the first time. You're always nervous going into a game, but the more you experience it, the better you become at dealing with it. I had spent the past few years getting a grasp of what pro baseball was all about, so when I took the mound in Seattle, I felt comfortable. One of the memories I have of this night was facing my old friend and Texas teammate Spike Owen soon after entering into the game. Spike, by this time, was a well-established and respected shortstop, and as he approached the box, I gave him a nod and a smile, as did he, in recognition of our history together. Then it was on. I knew if given the chance, he would show the crowd just how strong our friendship was by pounding a home run off me, just as he knew I would demonstrate those same feelings by striking his ass out. It ended up being a fly out and later on in the game, I would get a strikeout against him. I like to think of that as payback for knocking Westlake out of the state playoffs back in high school. All kidding aside, I pitched well in my first game, throwing three innings, giving up one run, and having a good visit with Spike afterward. I had my first real taste of getting to play without being overwhelmed by the Big League stage. It was all about experience and being comfortable with the surroundings, and I had crossed that threshold against Seattle.

I played in several more games on the West Coast swing, all as middle relief, and by the time we returned to Boston, I had pitched ten innings and given up only one run, which was during my first outing. This was just the start I was hoping for. When we arrived back, I had an opportunity to catch my breath and get acclimated to my new surroundings. Boston's Fenway Park is one of the meccas of professional sports. As the oldest active ballpark in the country, all-time greats like Ted Williams and Babe Ruth once called it home. If getting the walk-through of the stadium wasn't awe-inspiring enough, when I received my locker assignment, I noticed Tom Seaver occupied the locker next to mine. Yes, that Tom Seaver, the future Hall of Famer and one of the greatest pitchers in league history. The Red Sox had acquired him at mid-season to add depth to the pitching staff, and although he was at the end of his storied career, he was still formidable. What's more, he was a wonderful person who was easy to talk to and great to be around. With that said, being at Fenway and in the presence of legends like Seaver was indeed special, but I was at a critical point in my journey and by now was seasoned enough not to be distracted or overwhelmed by such things. My focus was solely on me doing the job they had sent me here to do. I was off to a good start and needed to maintain this mindset if I wanted to stay.

All continued to go well for me. Throughout July, I was pitching strong as a middle reliever, and it was beginning to get noticed. In fact, I was doing so well that they gave me a shot at being a closer, which is exactly where I wanted to be. The Red Sox were still leading the divisions, and every game from this point forward was important to reaching the postseason. This opportunity meant that I would be in a critical role at a meaningful time. Pitching in the majors was one thing, but doing it with so much on the line was quite another. Few ever get this chance.

My time came on August 3. We were playing the Kansas City Royals in Boston and were up 3–2 in the ninth inning. The Royals had runners at first and second with no outs when Mac called me in from the bullpen. The place was in a frenzy, but why wouldn't it be? After all, we're talking about Fenway Park filled to the rafters with Red Sox fans in the middle of a playoff run. To start it off, I would be facing the Royals' number three batter, Frank White, number four Steve Balboni, and number five Mike Kingery. I wasn't out there long. I got ahead of all of them, striking out the first two and grounding out the third to end the game. Fenway erupted, and I remember vividly just how good that moment felt. I had notched my first save in a Red Sox uniform, and up to that point, this was my biggest accomplishment as a pro. Since being called up, I had pitched fifteen innings with seventeen strikeouts and only given up one run. From August 9 to August 14, I appeared in four games and saved them all as we extended our division lead. I felt at home on the mound again, and there was a definitive buzz throughout Boston that the Red Sox may have found their new closer. It was all pretty cool.

About three weeks into August, in the locker room in Minnesota, Mac pulled me aside. He wanted to know what I thought about Spike Owen, what he was like as a player and a person. I told Mac that Spike was a great guy, one hell of a shortstop, and one of the best teammates I had ever played with. Without saying a word, Mac nodded his head and walked off, leaving me a little confused by his random inquiry. The next day, it was announced that Spike Owen and Dave Henderson were acquired in a trade with Seattle and would be joining us immediately. Snagging these guys meant we would have one of the best fielding shortstops in the game, along with the powerful bat of Dave Henderson as we made our run to the postseason. It was a great move and was the final puzzle piece for the 1986 Red Sox.

The team was hitting their stride, and we sat on top of the AL East with a somewhat comfortable four-game lead. I had never played better and was now the established closer. In the previous ten outings, I had an ERA of .4 and had thrown twenty-one consecutive scoreless innings. Roger was still on fire, and the talk of him winning the Cy Young Award was getting louder. Spike melded perfectly into our team and was everything Mac had hoped for and more. Don Baylor was playing like Don Baylor. It was around this time that some in the media began referring to the team as the Austin Red Sox since Roger, Spike, Don, and I all had strong ties to the city. It was a lot of fun, but that aside, as we entered the month of September, all focus was on winning the East and making it to the postseason. There was an unquestionable feel in the clubhouse that we were on the cusp of something special.

It had been eleven years since the Red Sox had won their division and sixty-seven years since they had won the World Series. In 1919, Boston was the most heralded baseball team in America. They had won the very first World Series and five of the first fifteen ever played. That year, owner Harry Freeze decided to send his best player, Babe Ruth, to the New York Yankees for $125,000, and as they say, the rest is history. Following that transaction, the Yankees would go on to be the most successful sports franchise in America, while the Red Sox, as of 1986, had never won another title. It was called the Curse of the Bambino, and although it wasn't commonly referred to as such until 1990, real or perceived, Red Sox fans were well aware of what that trade had done to both franchises. With that said, you can only imagine the excitement that surrounded our team. Bostonians were starving for a winner, something that this generation could call their own. Considering this, every home game brought out the full support of the city and energized one of the great fan bases in all the sports. I can tell you as a player, this created an incredible atmosphere, and playing in front of these fans was one of the great experiences of my life.

We kept our foot on the gas during the month of September, going 17–7. On September 22, Roger secured his twenty-fourth victory, all but clinching the Cy Young. It was a special moment for me, too, because I got the save, which allowed me to be part of such a monumental win with my old Texas teammate. The Red Sox were inching ever closer to the coveted AL East title, and on September 29, the long-awaited day finally arrived. Facing Toronto, Oil Can Boyd, who was having his best year, won his sixteenth game in front of the Fenway faithful, clinching the AL East title and sending us to the postseason. I have never experienced anything quite like Fenway Park immediately after that win. It was awe-inspiring to be a part of something that meant so much to the city and our fans.

* * *

Ebbs and flows inevitably come with each season, but the goal is always to be on the upside of these at the end. We were at this point and playing exceptional baseball going into the postseason. Wade Boggs, our third baseman, finished the regular season with a .357 batting average, earning him the coveted league batting title. Our starting pitching was phenomenal with Roger, Oil Can, and Hurst. Both offensively and defensively, we were peaking as well, with guys like Jim Rice, Don Baylor, Tony Armas, Dwight Evans, Dave Henderson, Spike, Bill Buckner, Rich Gedman, Marty Barrett, and Boggs all contributing at a high level. I was playing at a high level as well, and being a part of all of this had my confidence soaring higher than ever. I closed out the regular season with a 4–2 record, nine saves, and a 1.41 ERA. Mac was comfortable with putting me in tough situations, and I was comfortable with him doing it. I was the established closer for the AL East champions, we were headed to the playoffs, and it was all like living a dream.

Pitching for Boston. Making it through the gauntlet was great but I had far greater goals.

Chapter 8

AMERICAN LEAGUE CHAMPIONSHIP SERIES

If you are just tuning in, too bad.
—AL MICHAELS, ABC announcer, Game 5 ALCS

THE '86 POSTSEASON was here, and the only obstacle standing between us and a trip to the World Series was the AL West Champion
California Angels. They won ninety-two games that season, but we
won ninety-five, so home-field advantage for the American League
Championship Series belonged to the Boston Red Sox. The playoffs
are a best of seven series, so home field meant the first two games
were in Boston, followed by the next three in California, and then if
needed, a return to Boston for the final two. On the National League
side, my old team, the New York Mets, who had the best record in
baseball, faced off against the Houston Astros, winners of the NL
West, with Mike Scott as their ace. The Mets racked up a staggering 108 games that season, winning their division by an unheard-of

twenty-one games. In fact, all four playoff teams won their divisions by at least five games, which offered little drama in the regular season's closing days. Since baseball fans across America were denied any close divisional races down the stretch, anticipation for the playoffs hit a fever pitch. Besides that, these playoffs had all the ingredients of being something special, but nobody could have predicted just how special they would be. When all was said and done, 1986 would be considered the most famous postseason in Major League Baseball history.

October 7 was a beautiful fall evening in Boston, Massachusetts. The anticipation of playoff baseball was in the air, and you could practically feel the electricity surrounding the hallowed ground of Fenway Park. The major league postseason has a wholly unique feel—different from anything I had ever experienced. The adrenaline, the pressure, and the excitement were all dialed up to a higher level, and when our team took the field against the Angels, the energy felt by everyone was unmistakable. Clemens was on the mound for us, and Mike Witt, an eighteen game-winner, took the mound for California. These were two incredible pitchers playing exceptional baseball, so the matchup couldn't have been any better or more anticipated. The game started out much as planned, with both Roger and Witt each holding their opponents scoreless in the first.

In the second inning, the tide began to turn against us as the Angels pounded out three hits and took advantage of three walks to score four runs. They scored another in the middle of the third to go up 5–0, and by the time Roger had gotten the last guy out, he had already thrown almost ninety pitches. This was a nightmare scenario for us, and Witt made damn sure we never recovered. He pitched a gem that evening, keeping us off balance the entire night; in the end, we got our asses kicked, 8–1. Fenway, the town, the players, and everyone associated with the Red Sox were shell-shocked as they left the stadium. Of course, everyone was aware that this was only the first of a seven-game series, but the fact that the Angels won it so handily in Boston (and roughed up Clemens in the process) was cause for great concern.

Boston and California are on opposite sides of the country. Fenway is just a stone's throw from the Atlantic Ocean, and Anaheim Stadium is just a stone's throw from the Pacific. The cities are almost 3,000 miles apart, which has always made it difficult for road teams from the respective coasts to win. So, in short, losing Game 1 at home was a really big deal. Losing Game 2 at home would all but seal our fate, and we knew it as we suited up to play the very next afternoon. We put Bruce Hurst on the mound against Kirk McCaskill, a seventeen-game winner. After Hurst held the Angels scoreless in the first inning, our leadoff batter, Wade Boggs, hit a triple and set the tone for the entire game. It was interesting for a while, but eventually, we broke it open in the later innings and won 9–2. Bruce gave up eleven hits, but they were scattered throughout and inflicted no real damage. He provided just the performance we needed, and now we had to travel to the West Coast for three games. If we failed to win at least one of them, we would never make it back to Fenway, and our season would be over.

Anaheim Stadium is a beautiful ballpark and was filled to its capacity of 65,000 for Game 3. Sammy Davis Jr opened the show with a beautiful rendition of the National Anthem. We started our flamboyant yet incredibly talented pitcher, Oil Can Boyd, who had won sixteen games that year. California went with John Candelaria, who came to the Angels in a late-season trade and went on to win ten games. Both pitched well that day. In the second inning, Rich Gedman gave us the lead with an RBI, and we carried a 1–0 lead all the way to the sixth. Mr. October, Reggie Jackson, tied the game for them with an RBI in the sixth, and then they got us for three runs in the seventh to take a 4–1 lead. In the top of the eighth, the Angels replaced Candelaria with Donnie Moore, who had been their top closer for some time. Donnie was really good but had been hampered by shoulder issues which required him to get cortisone shots throughout the season, including one the night before this game, so nobody really knew what to expect when he took the mound. As it turned out, Moore balked in a run, gave up another, and we closed their lead to 4–3.

In the bottom of the eighth, Mac pulled Oil Can, and I was called in from the bullpen. I hadn't pitched in a week, so it was important to get out there and get acclimated to playoff baseball. Of course, I was nervous, but I was also pumped to be out there and felt totally in control of my mind and my pitching. The first batter flew out to short (which really helped settle things down), and next up was Reggie. He calmly strolled toward the batter's box. I pitched him well, eventually getting to a full count. I followed with a great pitch that he took, and it was right there, but I didn't get the call, and Jackson got the walk. Batter wins. I didn't show it outwardly, but I was absolutely livid about the call. Instead of two outs with nobody on, I had one out with a man on first and was facing my first stressful inning in the playoffs.

The term "stressful inning" is understood in baseball circles and used as a kind of measurement to describe the potential toll that an inning takes on a pitcher, both physically and mentally. It doesn't show up in the stats sheets or on any type of record, but it's real and is something of which the manager and pitcher are acutely aware. The term "stress," in this case, is not what you may think it is. It doesn't describe the external pressures brought about by the crowd or the game. Instead, stress refers to the situation within the inning that the pitcher faces while on the mound. For instance, if the pitcher retires three batters without allowing anyone to get on base, that would be considered a "stress-free" inning, despite the fact that it may have occurred under enormous pressure in the late stages of a very big game and in front of a boisterous crowd. Even if a runner gets on first with two outs and you get the next guy out, this is still considered a stress-free inning. What makes an inning "stressful" in the context to which I am referring is when runners get on base early in the inning with either no outs or one out. When this occurs, the whole dynamic of pitching changes, and the pitcher has to keep the runners out of scoring position. If they get into scoring position, the man on the mound must keep them from reaching home plate. This situation brings bunting into play. It makes routine fly balls more meaningful, makes passed balls much more costly—and most importantly, it forces the pitcher to pay attention to the base runners, diverting his focus from the task at hand. All of this occurs in the middle of the chess match between the batter and the pitcher, making it a stressful situation or inning. We all understand that the gold standard for monitoring a pitcher is the pitch count, but I can assure you that these stress situations can take a toll on a pitcher every bit as much as the pitch count. In other words, one stressful inning could have the same physical and mental impact that three stress-free innings do and sometimes more, depending upon the circumstance.

With Jackson on first, the next batter was Doug DeCinces, who I quickly got in front of 0-2. On the next pitch, he hit a potential inning-ending, double play ground ball that went between Boggs' legs and brought Reggie all the way around to third base. Batter wins. Boggs makes that play ninety-nine out of one hundred times, but shit like this happens, and you have to move on. The next guy hit a line drive to right-center, and Tony Armas made an incredible diving play to get him out, but Reggie tagged up and scored, giving the Angels a 5–3 lead. This was a great example of the defense saving the pitcher's ass because a lot of damage would have been done had that ball made it past Tony. The next guy flew out to left, and the inning was over. Although a run had been scored, I threw really well in regards to control, tempo, and velocity. Most importantly, I had experienced a stressful inning in the playoffs. All we needed now was a ninth-inning rally, but unfortunately for the Red Sox, Donnie Moore made sure that didn't happen and closed us out for a 5–3 win. What Donnie did was impressive. He had a very rough, stressful situation in the eighth, and yet, amidst the home crowd rumbling, managed to gather himself and get out of that pressure-packed situation in the ninth. Hats off to him. As far as the Red Sox, we were down 2–1 with two more to play in California. Game 3 was frustrating because, throughout the contest, we had opportunities to win but didn't do it. This turned Game 4 into an (almost) must-win situation for us because only one team in the history of the ALCS had ever come back from a 3–1 deficit. We had to find a way to stay out of that scenario.

Game 4 matched Roger, who was on three day's rest after throwing 143 pitches in Game 1, against Don Sutton, who had won fifteen games that year and a total of 300 in his Hall of Fame career. It was a classic pitcher's duel, as you might expect, and the Red Sox carried a 1–0 lead into the top of the eighth inning. By this time, Sutton was out, and we added two runs to take a 3–0 lead into the bottom half of the inning. Roger was still in the game and throwing well. Although Rupert Jones would take the first pitch of the eighth inning down the right-field line for a double, Clemens closed out the next three batters, and we entered the ninth holding on to a 3–0 lead. The Angels held us scoreless in the top of the ninth, but we were three outs away from tying the series with Roger still on the mound. Their first batter, Doug DeCinces, smashed the second pitch of the inning over the center-field wall for a home run, cutting our lead to 3–1. Hendricks then grounded out, followed by a Scofield base hit to left. Next, Bob Boone's base hit put runners on first and second with one out. That was it for Roger. Mac pulled him and called me in from the bullpen. There's no denying that this was a tense situation, but I had experienced it many times that season and was excited for the chance to close out the game. Gary Pettis was the first batter, and he hit a shot to left that Jim Rice initially lost in the lights. By the time he recovered and went back for it, the ball dropped over his head, scoring one run and leaving runners on second and third with one out.

Our lead narrowed to 3–2. We intentionally walked the next guy to load the bases and give ourselves an opportunity for a double play. Grich was the batter, needing only a base hit to end the game. I got him down in the count, 1–2, and then zipped a fastball by him for a strikeout and the second out. This was big because it meant that the defense could playback to their normal position. It would all come down to me and Brian Downing with a hell of a lot at stake. I blew the first two pitches right past him and went up 0–2, putting us one strike away from tying the series. I missed the next pitch high for a ball, and the count stood at 1–2. My catcher, Rick Gedman, flashed me the sign for a fastball, but I called him off that and went with a curve. The curveball was not the best pitch in my arsenal, but I knew

Downing wouldn't be expecting, so that's why I waved off Gedman. I let the 1–2 pitch go, but I started it way too far inside, which gave it no chance to get back around. I hit him in the leg, which scored the tying run. I repeat, I hit a batter on a 1–2 pitch with bases loaded, and the noise in Anaheim stadium was numbing. People can say whatever they want, but all I know is that on the mound, I was in total control before throwing that pitch. I just hung it out there too far, and it was very costly. My mistake was throwing that stupid ass curveball in the first place. This is where it gets real because you have to recompose yourself and get the next guy out, or the game is over. Yes, considering the situation, that's every bit as daunting as you think it is. The crowd was on its feet, and their roar was deafening as Reggie Jackson stepped up to the plate with bases loaded and the game tied at three. Everyone in Anaheim Stadium—all 65,000 of them—were anticipating Mr. October ending this thing. I blew a fastball by him to go 0–1, followed by a ball, and on the third pitch, he grounded out to second base to end the inning. There was a lot of damage done, but we were still in it and headed for extra innings.

The Angels held us scoreless in the top of the tenth, and the first batter I faced in the bottom was Doug DeCinces. He flew out to center, followed by Hendrick (who I struck out), and then Dick Schofield popped out to right. It was a nine-pitch, one, two, three stress-free inning, and precisely what we needed to settle things down. California held us scoreless again in the top half of the eleventh, and I went back out to the mound to face their back-up catcher Jerry Narron, who I quickly got down 0–1, only to allow him a base hit to right field. Gary Pettis followed with a sacrifice bunt, moving Narron to second, so now the winning run was in scoring position with one out. We intentionally walked Rob Wilfong for a double play opportunity, and Bobby Grich was next up. I threw him a fastball with my first pitch, and he sent it to left field for a base hit. The runner scored from second, and the game was over. In an instant, the nightmare scenario we were desperately trying to avoid happened, and the Red Sox were down 3–1 in the series. As the Angels' dugout emptied and the celebration was carrying on around me,

I remember walking to the dugout, sitting down, and burying my face in a towel. As I sat there with my face hidden from view, all I could think about was throwing that stupid-ass curve in the ninth inning with the game on the line. It was a terrible decision, and it cost us big. The weight of the world was on me at that moment. Not only had I let down my teammates, I had let down Red Sox fans across the nation. It was as devastated as I had ever felt. In the locker room, several of my teammates suggested that I get to the training room to avoid the onslaught of media that began to pour in, but I decided against that and faced every one of them. The way I saw things, I had caused this mess, and running from those guys wasn't going to make it go away. Besides that, Game 5 was less than twenty-four hours away, and maybe facing the press would help bring some closure to this awful evening.

Facing the reporters didn't help close shit because afterward, I went back to the hotel, still numb from what had transpired hours before. Deb was with me, sitting quietly and helplessly because she knew there was nothing she could say that would relieve my pain. It was tough on her, as it is with all professional athletes' wives forced to deal with situations like this. It's difficult because they are sane enough to know that it's just a game, yet they are also sane enough to know that they could never get their husbands to believe it, especially at a time like this. With that in mind, we sat there motionless and stared at the walls. I then reached into my bag and got out my Bible. Now, I wouldn't consider myself to be the most religious person in the world, but I read the Bible every night before I went to bed. I always leave a marker to let me know where I left off the night before and when I flipped the pages to get to that night's reading, it was on Romans 5:3-5:

> *Not only so, but we also glory in our sufferings, because we know that suffering produces perseverance; perseverance, character; and character, hope. And hope does not put us to shame because God's love has been poured out into our hearts through the Holy Spirit, who has been given to us.*

I shook my head in disbelief that this was the passage awaiting me that evening. It brought me great comfort in an incredibly trying time. It also put the entire situation into perspective. I turned off the lights, laid my head on the pillow with my eyes wide open, and reflected on what I had just read. It was now well past midnight, and as I laid there, still wide awake, the phone rang. For obvious reasons, all outside calls are blocked from reaching players' rooms, so, to this very day, I don't know how in the hell this one got through. I picked up the phone, and a guy on the other end said, "Is this Calvin Schiraldi?" I replied, "Yes, it is." He then proceeded to tell me that he was a firefighter from San Francisco and that he had just watched the game with his buddies. Rather than just hanging up, I decided to take the abuse because the way I was feeling, I deserved every bit of it.

To my surprise, he introduced himself as David Jones, and he told me not to get down on myself and that he wanted me to know that he and his buddies at the firehouse were praying for me. These were California fans, mind you. Baffled by it all, I thanked him and gently hung up the phone. As I laid there in utter disbelief, I couldn't help but be uplifted by such an act of kindness that came out of nowhere. Once again, how that call got through, I'll never know, but I sure am glad it did because it did me a world of good. The phone call and the Scripture passage brought clarity to the situation, and I can say without hesitation that my perspective on baseball had changed. Looking back over my life, this was one of the most special moments, and it followed right after one of the darkest experiences I ever faced.

I finally got some sleep, which was a good thing because Game 5 was the next afternoon, and we were only twelve hours away from start time. When morning came, and we made our way to the stadium, the reality of the situation set in. Only one team in the history of baseball had ever come back from being down 3-1 in the ALCS, so in essence, my decision to throw that curveball had delivered a death blow to the team. Despite that reality, the Angels hadn't won the pennant yet, and we sure as hell weren't going to just give it to them. As dire as the situation was, we knew that if we could win Game 5 and get the series back to Fenway, the pressure would be back on them. Easier said than done, perhaps, but it represented the only hope we had.

It was a gorgeous day, seventy-eight degrees, with a blue sky overhead for Game 5 of the ALCS. On the mound for us was Bruce Hurst, who was at his very best; and for the Angels, it was one of the hottest pitchers in baseball, Mike Witt, who had been brilliant in his Game 1 victory. While Anaheim was off the charts in anticipation of the Angels winning a trip to the World Series, Red Sox fans across the nation knew ours was a do-or-die situation. As they introduced the teams and sang the National Anthem, I think everyone expected a good game, but no one could have predicted just how great it would be.

The game started with both teams held scoreless in the first. In the second, with Rice on first, Gedman hit a home run to right field to give us an early 2–0 lead. The Angels scored a run in the third, making it 2–1, and we held that lead all the way to the bottom of the sixth. Hurst was dominating this inning for us, but with two outs, two strikes, and nobody on, the Angels' Doug DeCinces hit a double to the right-field wall. Then, with two strikes also, Grich sent a deep fly ball to the wall while Dave Henderson, running full speed, chased it down and leaped for it. Dave actually had the ball in his glove for the final out, but when he hit the wall, arm fully extended, the impact jarred the ball loose, and it fell over the fence for a two-run homer. Batter wins. It was an unbelievably bad break on what would have been a spectacular play by Dave. The sixth ended, and we were now down 3–2, but more importantly for the Angels, the crowd was now fully engaged, and their first World Series in franchise history appeared inevitable.

We replaced Hurst with Bob Stanley in the seventh, and they picked up two more runs extending their lead to 5–2 as the energy inside Anaheim Stadium soared to a monumental level. We didn't score in the eighth, and thankfully, neither did they. Stanley's performance that inning was critical because any additional runs for them would have reduced our already small chance of winning to almost nothing. We headed into the ninth, just three outs away from elimination and down three runs. What made the task before us damn near impossible was the fact that Witt was still in the game and pitching extremely well. This made being down by three feel like we were down by ten. I was in the bullpen in left field watching the game unfold, and the scene around me, to put it delicately, began to deteriorate. The fans were unmerciful and mocked me for the previous game's performance in ways I have never experienced. I guess that was to be expected. Something else, however, was happening in left field, and this wasn't expected. In fact, it was bizarre. Securing the area in and around the bullpen were several mounted police officers assigned the task of keeping rowdy fans from storming the field after the inevitable Angels victory. As their horses crapped all over the place, these cops verbally crapped all over me. Right in lockstep with the fans seated outside the bullpen, these cops were wearing my ass out. They taunted me about losing the game the night before and talked shit like you wouldn't believe. That's right, police officers on horseback talking shit to the players. It was like being in another world.

The ninth inning got underway, and Bill Buckner led off with a base hit. Jim Rice followed but unfortunately struck out. The Angels were now only two outs away. Witt had a full count on Don Baylor and threw a nasty pitch. Somehow, Baylor got a bat on it and took that ball out of the yard for a two-run home run. Batter wins. Interviewed later, Witt said he would have thrown that pitch a hundred more times, and Baylor would never have hit a home run off of it. That should give you some idea of just how good Baylor's swing was. This two-run shot helped calm the chaos a bit and made our glimmer of hope somewhat brighter, albeit it very little. We were now down 5–4 with one out, and Witt forced Dwight Evans to pop out to third. They were one out away with Rich Gedman up and the stadium going absolutely nuts again. This was when it got interesting. Gedman had hit Witt hard all game, so the Angels made the decision to pull Witt, who was just one out away from a complete game, and bring in Gary Lucas. The move stirred some controversy, but Lucas had dominated Gedman in the past, so at least in those terms, it made sense.

As it turned out, Lucas struck Gedman with the very first pitch, sending Rich to first and ending Lucas' short time on the mound. With two outs and a runner on first, the Angels brought in Donnie Moore to face Dave Henderson in what would become one of the most famous at-bats in history. Moore was throwing well, and although his first pitch was a ball, he followed it with one of his patented fastballs to go 1–1. On his next throw, he picked up his second strike and was now one away from sending the Angels to their first World Series ever. Back in the left-field bullpen, the shit storm raining down on me had subsided after the Baylor home run but now roared back with a vengeance. The horses were ready to storm the field along with the fans, and everyone in the stadium was on their feet. It was so loud you couldn't hear the person next to you. At home plate and down in the count 1–2, Dave fouled off the next three pitches, which were all really good, to stay alive. On the seventh pitch, Moore threw a nasty forkball, but Henderson reached for it, made good contact, and sent it toward left-center field. The center fielder went back for it, but it just kept going, eventually clearing the wall for a two-run homer. Batter wins. This gave us a 6–5 lead, and I can report to you from the bullpen that the Clint Eastwood wannabes on horseback weren't talking shit anymore. In fact, nobody was. The place fell completely silent.

The Moore/Henderson at-bat only lasted seven pitches but embodied everything I described about the chess match between pitcher and batter. Donnie had him off balance the entire time, but Dave fought masterfully just to stay alive and allow himself a chance. He then capitalized on the only pitch Moore gave him, which was still nasty, and won the match. Considering they both performed at that level with so much on the line tells you everything you need to know about the winning spirit inside both men. It was a beautiful thing to witness. As he faced the next batter, Moore, demonstrating incredible mental toughness, recomposed himself and limited further damage by getting an out to end the inning. The odds had completely flipped in our favor as we entered the bottom of the ninth up 6–5. Needless to say, Anaheim Stadium was completely silent, if not in absolute shock.

It was now our turn to get it done as we were just three outs away from moving this series back to Boston. Bob Stanley took the mound for us, pitching to the Angels' Bob Boone, who delivered with a base hit to center field. Gary Pettis followed that up with a sacrifice bunt, moving Boone to second with one out. Mac then pulled Stanley and brought in Joe Sambito to face the Angels' Rob Wilfong. The first pitch was a base hit, and the game tied up at 6–6. The crowd rose to their feet, and just like that, the Red Sox were on the ropes again. As we faced elimination, Steve Crawford, who inherited one out and a runner on first, replaced Sambito. The previous July, Crawford was the guy put on injured reserve, providing me with the opportunity to join the Red Sox. He was a good reliever but hadn't played much since returning, making this a brutal situation to be thrown into. Crawford got Angels' batter Dick Schofield down 0–1 but then gave up a base hit to put runners at first and third with one out. The next batter was intentionally walked, loading the bases. Back in the bullpen, "Clint Eastwood" and his mounted gang of uniformed trash talkers had reclaimed the territory around me. It was on again with everyone jeering and mocking us more intensely than they had all day. I don't wish to belabor the point, but it was the damnedest thing I ever witnessed. With bases loaded, deafening crowd noise, and everything on the line, Crawford faced DeCinces. On the very first pitch, Crawford got him to fly out to shallow right, denying the Angels' base runners an opportunity to tag, and more importantly, giving us the precious second out. Bobby Grich came up next and fought Crawford to 2–2, but on the next pitch, he got jammed and hit a soft shot back to Crawford, who caught it, ending the ninth. We were headed for extra innings. Steve had done an exceptional job battling out of that situation and the crowd at Anaheim, once again, fell silent.

In the tenth, Moore was still in for the Angels and began the inning by walking Wade Boggs. Marty Barrett tried a sacrifice bunt, but the first baseman threw out Boggs at second. Stapelton then got a hit to right field, sending Barrett to third. We now had a runner on first and third with one out and Jim Rice at the plate. Moore threw a good pitch, and Rice hit a grounder to short for a double play to end the inning. Unfortunately, we had missed on a golden opportunity, and the momentum and the crowd were now back on the Angels' side.

Still in for us in the bottom of the tenth, Steve Crawford got Reggie Jackson to ground out for the first out. He then struck out White for the second out and walked Narron, putting him on first. Gary Pettis was up next, and with two outs and a runner on first, he absolutely smashed a 3–2 pitch, sending Rice all the way to the wall where he made an outstanding catch at the top of the fence. It was literally inches from being a series-winning home run. Pitcher wins, inning over. If that ball had gone out, I'm not sure how I would have escaped the Eastwood gang or Angel fans in left field because the frenzied chaos which would have ensued would have been completely out of control. With that said, this was now the most unbelievable game I have ever seen, and it was still far from over as we moved on to the eleventh.

In the top of the inning, the Angels' Donnie Moore faced his first batter, Don Baylor, and hit him with a pitch. A base hit from Evans followed, while an exceptional Gedman bunt for a single loaded the bases with no outs. The inning could have been considerably worse for the Angels, but they got out of it only giving up one run. We scored when Dave Henderson hit a sacrifice fly to center to send Baylor home. The momentum had reverted back to us, and we were once again three outs away from ending it, leading 7–6.

Heading into the bottom of the eleventh inning, Mac signaled to the bullpen, calling on me to close the game. It was one of life's rare moments when you get a shot at redemption, and for the second time in my baseball career, I was being afforded it. Motivated by the night before, the present bullpen chaos with all that shit being aimed my way, and most of all, an opportunity to help our team get back to Boston, I stepped out of the bullpen. As I did so, and in terms they would clearly understand, I bid farewell to the "Eastwood gang" and left field fans. As fate would have it, I would be facing the same three batters as I had in that devastating inning the night before. You couldn't write a better script. This situation offered me two outcomes—either I would find redemption, or I was going to get cemented into infamy. All that mattered to me was the chance to do either. I started out against Rob Wilfong, and my first pitch was a strike. After three pitches, I was sitting on a 1–2 count. I threw a fastball by him, striking him out for the first out.

Next up was Schofield, who I got down early and struck out with five pitches for out number two. Finally, it was Brian Downing, who I had hit the night before with that ill-advised curveball. My first pitch was a strike, and then he took two straight balls. I threw the next pitch by him, and the count stood at 2–2. Here we were again, one strike away, and he sure as hell wasn't going to see my curveball this time. I let loose a fastball which he popped up foul between home plate and first. Dave Stapelton made an easy catch directly in front of me, finally ending this epic game.

We were going back to Boston, and as the catch was made, I remember leaping in the air about eleven inches (as it turned out). The stunned crowd went completely silent as the Red Sox emptied the dugout and celebrated unconstrained on their field. As the dust settled, it was clear that this game epitomized what sports are all about: two divisional champions demonstrated an unbelievable will to win, leaving everything they had on the field. The player's, the fans in attendance, and the national television audience immediately recognized that they had just witnessed one for the ages—and they weren't wrong. Game 5 of the 1986 ALCS would go down as one of the greatest playoff games ever played, and getting to be a part of it was very, very special.

After celebrating in the locker room, doing interviews, and showering, we boarded the bus and headed for the airport. The flight back to Boston was one of the best experiences of my life. I'd like to say that we were watching film or going over strategy for Game 6, but that didn't happen. What did happen was an epic, all-out party, taking place at 35,000 feet as we crossed the United States. I won't elaborate any further, but trust me, the trip home was legendary.

Although we were still down 3–2 when we arrived at Fenway for Game 6, we all knew that in order to beat us, the Angels had two distinct disadvantages to overcome. First, there was the travel. As I mentioned before, it's hard as hell to travel across the country and win a game. Jet lag, hotel rooms, and just being far from home negatively impact ballplayers. Another problem the Angels had to overcome was the devastating home loss back in California. In sports, getting over something of that magnitude is easier said than done. We pitched Oil Can that night, and although he gave up two runs in the first, he threw exceptionally well. Additionally, our bats came alive, especially in the fifth inning, where we scored five runs to blow the game wide open. Bob Stanley closed it for Oil Can in the ninth, and we won the game, 10–4. The series was now tied, 3–3, with the winner of Game 7 headed to the World Series. We would have to face John Candelaria, which would be tough, but they would have to face Roger Clemens, the best pitcher in the major leagues.

If you had to find the perfect setting for a Game 7 in the ALCS, Fenway Park on a crisp October evening would be a pretty good place to start. The atmosphere surrounding this game was similar to that in California before Game 5, the only difference being that this time, it was a stadium full of devoted Boston fans desperately anticipating a trip to the World Series. The energy pulsating throughout Fenway was nothing short of incredible. On that evening, Roger demonstrated why he was so worthy of the 1986 Cy Young Award. He lasted seven innings, giving up only four hits the entire night. We scored three runs in the second and then, highlighted by a Jim Rice three-run homer, blew it wide open in the fourth with four runs. In the eighth inning, with no outs and a runner on first, Mac pulled Roger, who strolled toward the dugout with an 8–0 lead.

Fenway erupted, giving him a rousing standing ovation that lasted for minutes. Recalling that moment still gives me chills. Mac called me in from the bullpen, and there I stood on the mound in front of the frenzied Red Sox faithful, six outs away from the World

Series. Nothing can properly prepare a ballplayer for a moment like this, and between the nerves and the excitement, it's difficult to describe exactly how I felt.

With a runner on first, my first pitch went for a bloop single that fell just beyond Barrett's reach, giving them runners on first and second and still no outs. I then struck out Downing with three pitches. The next batter up was Reggie Jackson, and although he was closing in on the twilight of his career, he was still dangerous as hell. If anyone could provide the Angels with the spark they desperately needed, it was Mr. October. I got him down 1–2, then he fouled two pitches off, and finally, I threw a fastball by him, striking him out. With two outs, Doug DeCinces came up next, and I got him down 1–2 before he smashed one off the Green Monster for a long single that scored a run. The next batter flew out to right field, and the top half of the inning was over. The Red Sox were three outs away from the World Series.

Just like the state championship tournament in high school or going to Omaha in college, the World Series represents the pinnacle of professional baseball. But unlike the other two, the World Series is the highest point of the highest mountain, making it the ultimate dream of anyone who has ever played this game. Getting there is one of the rarest feats in sports, and having played this game since I was a child, I understood this as much as anyone. In the top of the ninth, I faced Gary Pettis and struck him out looking. The next batter, I struck out as well for out number two. Fenway Park was rocking, and I mean that literally.

Everyone in the stands was on their feet, and they created so much noise that you could actually feel the place shaking. With two outs and facing Jerry Narron, I threw three adrenaline-fueled pitches, including the last one, which he swung at and missed. I struck out the side to end the game. I don't remember much after that, but I do recall the exhilaration inside of that stadium as everyone went completely crazy.

• • •

The Boston Red Sox were going to the World Series, and no amount of words could possibly describe what Fenway was like at that moment. Marty Barrett was named ALCS MVP for his consistently stellar performance throughout all seven games. The celebration in Boston, which swept up most of the Red Sox players, too, continued throughout the night. It was a once-in-a-lifetime experience— a special time indeed. As for baseball fans across the country and around the world, they had the privilege of witnessing an epic series, one so good that it has earned the distinction as one of the best American League Championship Series ever played.

AP PHOTO

AP PHOTO / Rod Boren

The expression says it all after hitting the batter in Game 4 of the ALCS. I still can't believe I threw that stupid ass curve in that situation. After Game 4, that was a tough time to get through.

On the mound closing out the Angels in Game 5 of the ALCS. I only wish I had a picture of the Eastwood gang that had me surrounded in the bullpen.

DAVID MADISON / Getty Images Sport

THE SHOT HEARD AROUND THE BASEBALL WORLD
Dave Henderson rounding the bases in front of a shocked crowd at
Anaheim Stadium.

AP PHOTO / Reed Saxon

Dave and me walking off the field at Game 5 of the ALCS. A huge win for
Red Sox Nation.

AP Photo / Paul Benoit

Celebrating after after striking out the side in Game 7 of the ALCS. Roger threw a masterpiece and I closed it.

Engulfed by my teammates as we celebrated our ticket to the World Series.

Chapter 9

1986 WORLD SERIES

You don't just accidentally show up in the World Series.
—DEREK JETER

NO WORDS could possibly describe what it was like knowing that I was going to play in the World Series. Any boy who was ever serious about baseball can only dream of such a chance. Our opponent was none other than my old team, the New York Mets, who were considered the best team in baseball and heavily favored to win it all. They had defeated the Houston Astros in the National League Championship Series in six games, with the last one requiring sixteen innings to resolve. Although I can't say I saw much of it, it was reported that the NLCS was every bit as epic as our Series with the Angels. Bob Ojeda, who was involved in the trade with me at the end of 1985, was enjoying an outstanding year on the mound, winning Game 2 of the NLCS. Ours would be one of many storylines spotlighted during the 1986 World Series. In truth, this contest didn't need any quirky storylines because it was Boston vs. New York, and the disdain these cities had for each other's team dates back to the beginning of baseball itself.

For me, it was no surprise that the Mets were as good as they were in 1986. As I mentioned, for several years, their minor league teams had dominated Single-A, Double-A, and Triple-A baseball. They were flush with incredible young talent, most of whom I had the privilege to play with and witness firsthand just how good they were. What's more, the Mets had several damn good veteran players to complement their youth, and in 1986, this perfect mixture of young and old evolved into a synergy that created a team that doesn't come around very often. Considering this, the fact that they had the best record in baseball made sense and earned the Mets home-field advantage in the World Series. Having to potentially play four of the seven games in New York was a big deal, but it wasn't nearly as bad as it could have been because New York is only an hour and a half flight from Boston. That at least took jet lag out of the equation. Travel time or not, we would still have to play in Shea Stadium, which wasn't so bad—if you were wearing a Mets jersey (as I was the year before). Entering that place in a Boston uniform now meant facing the wrath of their fans, and I knew how much of an advantage that gave the Mets. On the other hand, let's not forget that they would have to come to Fenway for three games, and trust me, that was no picnic for anyone wearing a Mets jersey. Although all of the experts had them as heavy favorites to win the Series, we knew we could beat anyone, and so did our fans.

On October 18, Game 1 of the 1986 World Series got underway on a chilly night in New York. Ron Darling, who had won fifteen games that year, was on the mound for the Mets and Bruce Hurst was on the mound for us. Both pitchers were remarkable that evening, so much so that the game was scoreless going into the seventh inning. With Jim Rice on second and one out in the top of the seventh, Rich Gedman hit a grounder to second that went through Tim Teufel's legs. Rice scored on the error, and we led, 1-0. Darling finished the seventh, which would be his last of the game, having given up only three hits all night. After the eighth, Hurst left the game with no runs surrendered and only four hits allowed. It was a classic pitcher's duel worthy of a World Series opening game, that's for sure.

Headed into the bottom of the ninth, we were leading 1–0, and I was called in to close the game. I was taking the mound in the World Series at Shea Stadium and fulfilling every dream I ever had as a young kid. For a baseball player, this was as rare an opportunity as there was, and it came with unbridled excitement and unbridled pressure. It was nothing short of awesome.

It was pretty cold that night and a challenge for everyone to stay physically loose. I remember having to constantly blow into my pitching hand to keep it warm in order to properly grip the baseball. Surprisingly, the crowd hadn't really been a factor all evening, but that all changed when Daryl Strawberry came to the plate to open the inning. At that point, they awakened. Comebacks had been a Mets trademark throughout that season (forty-one times in fact), so as if on cue, the crowd rose to their feet in anticipation of another. I helped their cause and didn't do myself any favors by walking Strawberry with just five pitches. This stoked the crowd, and trust me—they made damn sure I felt it. Next up, Ray Knight bunted to advance Strawberry into scoring position, but our first baseman, Dave Stapelton, quickly fielded it and threw Strawberry out at second. It was a gutsy, high-risk, high-reward play by Dave and a huge out for us. We now had Knight at first with one out. Wally Backman was up next, and he battled five pitches to a full count.

The next pitch was hit to shallow left, and Rice caught it for out number two, still leaving Knight on first. Although I never remember experiencing the level of intensity that I did entering this game, I was now acclimated and couldn't have felt better. Danny Heep was the next batter, and I struck him out on four pitches to end the game and secure the 1–0 victory. You could hear a pin drop in Shea Stadium after that last out. Getting the save in the World Series was incredible, but most gratifying was preserving the win for Hurst, who had pitched an absolute gem. Winning at Shea to open the Series was a very big deal for us, proving that the Boston Red Sox could win anywhere against anyone. I was pitching well, and my confidence was sky-high. In my last three outings, Games 5 and 7 of the ALCS and Game 1 of the World Series, I had pitched four innings, struck out nine of fifteen batters faced, and gave up only two hits with one run. With the Red Sox up 1–0 in the Series, the Mets faced enormous pressure because losing two at home would put them in a hole that would be very hard to overcome.

Game 2 of the '86 World Series featured one of the most anticipated pitching matchups of the year: twenty-four-year-old Roger Clemens against twenty-two-year-old Dwight Gooden. Unfortunately for the fans, neither would make it past the fifth inning. Both Dwight Evans and Dave Henderson hit home runs for us, and Steve Crawford would get the win, 9–3. We had accomplished the unthinkable by winning both games at Shea, leaving the heavily favored Mets up against the wall. The World Series was headed to Fenway for a three-game stretch, and the Red Sox were up 2–0.

The Mets didn't back down in Game 3 and showed no indications of the pressure that came from being down 0–2. They smashed us 7–1, making an emphatic statement to us and the baseball world that they weren't going anywhere. They scored four runs in the first inning and never looked back as Bob Ojeda beat Oil Can to get their first victory and close the Series gap, 2–1. The next day, in Game 4, they rolled us again with Strawberry and Dykstra both hitting home runs and getting the win for Ron Darling over Al Nipper, 6–2. The Mets had accomplished an improbable feat, doing precisely what they needed to. The Series was now tied 2–2, but most importantly for the Mets, they had reclaimed home-field advantage. Coming into Fenway under those circumstances and doing what they did was impressive, to say the least.

It was the strangest and most unpredictable thing baseball had ever seen. Through four World Series games, neither team had won at home. The odds of this ever happening in any World Series were astronomical, but when you consider the distinct advantage Fenway and Shea home crowds offered their teams, the odds were almost non-existent. Nobody—and I mean nobody—could have predicted this scenario. After winning back-to-back games in Boston, the Mets had recaptured the momentum. As we entered our final game at Fenway, we found ourselves in a must-win situation because we knew, better than anyone, that this anomaly of the visitors winning these games was not sustainable. With our backs against the wall, we did what we had to do and won Game 5. This demonstrated to the Mets and the baseball world that the Red Sox weren't going away either. We pitched Hurst, and the Met's pitched Gooden. Bruce was masterful and threw a complete game to secure his second win of the Series, 4–2. More importantly, the victory gave us a 3–2 lead (and the momentum) as we headed back to Shea for the final two games, needing only one for the World Championship.

By now, the fan bases for the Red Sox and Mets weren't the only ones interested in what was transpiring. This epic dogfight between the two pennant winners was beginning to take on a life of its own. By the time Game 6 rolled around, the Series was the talk of the entire country. The World Series has always been a major draw, but the television network ratings in 1986 were through the roof and were about to become record-setting. To be an athlete in this situation was the stuff of dreams—two teams at the doorstep of greatness, both relentlessly clawing and fighting their way to the top, the ultimate prize on the line, and all before an audience of millions. I was twenty-four years old and in the middle of it, but I still can't do it justice today when describing what it was really like. No one can.

October 25, 1986, was a cold Saturday evening in New York. The pregame atmosphere inside Shea Stadium was like nothing I have ever seen. In fact, I think it is safe to say that none of the other players had either. I remember being on the field for the Red Sox warm-up about an hour before the game, and having to maneuver around a massive sea of reporters who had descended upon the field. It was a bizarre scene. They were everywhere, and we did our best to navigate the terrain while they barked out questions and requested pregame interviews. As game time approached, the reporters slowly dissipated, and the stands filled to capacity with hardcore Mets fans ready to unleash their rabid fury on the hated Red Sox. It's hard to imagine that the electricity in the air could be ramped up beyond what we had already experienced throughout the playoffs, but I can tell you firsthand that it had, and it was special.

Bob Ojeda took the mound for the Mets in the first inning. He faced our leadoff hitter, Wade Boggs, who opened the game with a single. Marty Barrett then flew out, and Bill Buckner came to the plate. While Buckner was ready to hit and Ojeda was looking for signals from the catcher, the umpire abruptly called time. Suddenly, the attention of everyone present focused on the skies above, where a parachutist descended slowly onto the infield. It was as funny as it was surreal, and everyone seemed to get some enjoyment out of it. After they took the uninvited guest away, the game was back on, and Ojeda got Buckner to pop out to Dykstra for out number two. Jim Rice followed with a walk, and then Dwight Evans came to the plate, blasting a double into the gap, scored Boggs, and gave us an early 1–0 lead. It was the perfect way to start the game, and it worked wonders settling us down and getting us acclimated.

Roger Clemens took the mound for us and struck out the first two batters, and quickly retired the third for a very quick 1–2–3 stress-free inning. Ojeda got in trouble again in the second, giving up hits to Spike, Boggs, and Barrett, surrendering another run, which gave us a 2–0 lead. Roger got all the way through the fourth without giving up a single hit, and after Ojeda made it through the top of the fifth with no damage, our lead stood at 2–0.

To open the bottom of the fifth, Roger walked Strawberry, who subsequently stole second. Ray Knight followed this with a base hit to score Strawberry and close the lead to 2–1. Mookie Wilson then got a hit to right field, which Dwight Evans didn't field cleanly and allowed Knight to go all the way to third. There were now runners on first and third with no outs. Roger got Danny Heep to hit into a double play, but Knight scored from third and tied the game, 2–2. This was followed by Bob Ojeda grounding out to end the fifth inning, but the crowd at Shea had officially come to life. Roger was damn near untouchable through four innings, so when they hit him the way they did in the fifth, it brought the stadium alive in ways I've never seen. It would remain that way for the rest of the game.

In the top of the seventh, Roger McDowell replaced Ojeda with the game still tied 2–2. He opened the inning by walking Barrett.

Buckner followed with a ground ball, but Barrett was stealing when it was hit and made it to second to spoil the double play. With one out, Jim Rice hit a routine grounder to Knight at third base, but Knight made a bad throw to first. With the ball sailing over Keith Hernandez's outstretched glove, Barrett reached third with Rice safe at first. This was a costly error, and Ray, more than anyone, knew it. With one out, the Mets were in a tough situation. Next up, Dwight Evans hit a grounder, but it coincided with Rice stealing second base, causing the Mets defenders to again miss out on a double play. Even worse for the Mets, Barrett scored from third. We had regained the lead, 3–2. With Rice on second and two outs, Rich Gedman got a base hit to left field. Waved on, Rice rounded third base in full stride. Mookie Wilson fielded the ball cleanly and let it loose toward home in what would be one of the game's critical moments. The throw from left field was absolutely perfect, and Gary Carter ended the inning by tagging out a sliding Rice at home plate. The play was nothing short of spectacular, especially when you consider the circumstances surrounding it and the damage that another run would have inflicted on the Mets. It was high-level baseball displayed by Mookie, that's for sure.

Clemens held the Mets scoreless in the bottom of the seventh, keeping his 3–2 lead. In the top of the eighth, Dave Henderson opened the inning with a base hit, followed by a successful Spike Owen bunt that advanced Dave to second. With one out and a runner in scoring position, Coach McNamara called on Mike Greenwell to pinch hit for Roger, which ended the night for Clemens. In the days, weeks, months, and years that followed, Mac's move would draw a lot of attention as people wondered why Roger was taken out and if he was coming out so that we could score Dave, why wasn't Baylor chosen to pinch-hit for him. None of this mattered to McDowell, however, because he had to face the next batter regardless of who it was, and as it turned out, he struck out Greenwell with some really nasty pitches. With Dave still on second and two outs, the Mets decided to intentionally walk Boggs. Remember, Boggs was the best hitter in baseball that year, and the Met's didn't want him swinging with a man in scoring position. McDowell then walked Marty Barrett, which wasn't intentional, and this loaded the bases for us. With two outs in the top of the eighth, they pulled McDowell and brought in Jesse Orosco to face Bill Buckner. A hit of any kind could spell the end for the Mets season, and I think everyone watching felt the importance of the moment. Bill made good contact on the very first pitch, but it was a fly ball to center field, and the Mets successfully fought themselves out of a very precarious situation. Heading into the bottom of the eighth, we were still clinging to a 3–2 lead.

I knew when Roger didn't hit in the top of the eighth that I'd be called into the game. It was a surreal moment, standing on the mound, six outs away from the World Championship. At this point, the crowd had been nuts since the fifth inning, so there was nothing shocking or overwhelming about the noise. What's more, it was similar to the situation I had just experienced seven days earlier when I got the save in Game 1. Same mound. Same fans. I was pitching extremely well going into this with my arm well-rested and feeling strong. In short, I was facing a once-in-a-lifetime opportunity, and although I was as nervous as anyone would be in this situation, I was equally thrilled to be out there.

With a 3–2 lead in the bottom of the eighth, the first batter I faced was Lee Mazzilli. He took the first pitch for a strike, fouled off the next one, and I was quickly ahead of him, 0–2. With the count at 1–2, he hit a ground ball that rolled between first and second for a base hit. I pitched him well, but anytime a batter makes contact, it can be a problem, and this was a perfect example. I now had a runner on first with no outs. Gedman and Buckner came to the mound to discuss strategy for the obvious bunting situation that we now faced. Dykstra was up next, and advancing the runner with a bunt would be his only objective. I threw him the pitch, and he laid it down to my right side. I ran for it and fielded it quickly enough to make a play for Mazzilli at second. I spun and let the ball loose towards Spike, but I threw it low, and Spike had to try and short hop it out of the dirt. He couldn't come up with it. Both runners were safe, and it would be an understatement to say that this was a bad situation. With no outs and runners on first and second, the Mets weren't through with the bunting game. Wally Backman was up next, and he squared up and bunted down the third-base line. I fielded it cleanly with plenty of time to get Mazzilli out at third, but when I went to make the throw, I noticed Boggs wasn't on third base. He had come in to field the bunt, and although he was scrambling to get back, there wasn't enough time, so I had to spin around and throw to first. Thankfully, my toss made it in time to get Backman out. This could have been disastrous had we not gotten somebody out on the play, and it was very close to happening. With runners on second and third, we intentionally walked Keith Hernandez. Now the bases were loaded with one out.

Do I need to waste your time by describing the atmosphere inside Shea Stadium at that moment? Just try to imagine it and then multiply that by thirty. Gary Carter was up next. My first pitch was really good and right there, but it was called a ball. I went inside with the next pitch and just missed it for ball two. Next, I went outside thinking he would be swinging, and he wasn't. I had thrown three consecutive balls with the bases loaded, and for a pitcher, the situation doesn't get any more nightmarish than that. Think about it. You can't walk him with the bases loaded, so obviously, you have to throw a strike, and throwing a strike to a guy like Carter, when he knows that it's coming, is not a pleasant position to be in. I did what I had to do, and he ripped a line drive right at Jim Rice in left field, who caught it and tried to get the tagging runner out at home plate. Mazzilli beat the throw, so now the game was tied 3–3, runners at second and third, and two outs. The lead was gone, which wasn't good, but this inning had disaster written all over it, so giving up the lead was the furthest thing from my mind. I'll describe to you what this moment felt like as I waited for the next batter. Other than getting behind Carter, I had pitched well this inning, and yet, I was in the midst of total chaos.

The run that scored was mine, the runners on second and third were mine, and I had only given up one hit. Worse yet, I was in a situation where if the next batter gets a hit, the game is likely over. The crowd was wearing my ass out, and through it all, I had to find enough composure to settle down and get the final out. It's a brutal way to make a living. If all of this wasn't bad enough, the next batter was Daryl Strawberry. I immediately got him down 0-2, which helped settle things down a bit. He popped the next pitch out to shallow center field, ending the most stressful inning of my life. Damage had been done, but it could have been so much worse, and we were still very much in it.

We moved to the ninth tied 3–3, and in the top half of the inning, they held us scoreless, so with a fresh start, I went back to the mound in the bottom. I'm going to refrain from describing the frenzy that awaited us as we took the field because I think you get it by now. Ray Knight came to the plate to start things off. I fell behind him 3–1 and eventually walked him. Ray was a tough guy to pitch to because he didn't strike out much and would wait you out until he got what he wanted. If he got what he wanted, he'd make you pay for it. Regardless, I had walked the leadoff batter, which meant that it was time to prepare for an onslaught of bunts, as they would try to put Knight in position to score the game-winning run. Mookie Wilson was up, and he took a strike. With the second pitch, he laid down a bunt that sat down right in front of Gedman, our catcher. Rich fielded it immediately and fired it to second, but his throw was high. Although Spike caught it, the umpire said that his foot had come off of the bag and called him safe. Barrett and Spike went ballistic, and Mac came flying out of the dugout to protest. From my perspective, it was damn close, and that's all I will say. After some heated words were exchanged, the call stood. Keep in mind that there was no replay in 1986, so getting this call overruled was not going to happen.

With no outs, I was now facing runners on first and second base, tied 3–3 in the bottom of the ninth inning of the World Series, and a base hit ends the game. Howard Johnson came up next looking to seal the game, but I struck him out on four pitches to get the first out. This was a big out, which released a ton of pressure. A lot of people wondered why Mets manager Davey Johnson didn't bunt Howard in that situation, but that wasn't my concern. All I knew is that Howard was swinging that bat with bad intentions and trying to end the game. With one out and runners on first and second, Lee Mazzilli was facing a 2–1 count and flew out to Rice in left field, leaving the runners with no chance to tag. We were one out from escaping the inning, but keep in mind—they were still one hit from winning the game.

The crowd was on their feet when Dykstra came to the plate. I got him down 0-1, and then he got it to 2–2. He took the next pitch, which was a ball, to make the count full. I then threw a good fastball which resulted in a fly out to Rice in left field. We had escaped the inning with no damage. This inning has kind of been lost to history, which is a shame because it was a grinding ordeal that offered true baseball fans everything they could want to see. I had walked Knight at the outset, and that became magnified when he was called safe at second. From that point forward, the inning was a true meat grinder, and with no outs and the game on the line with every swing, I had to get Johnson, Mazzilli, and Dykstra out, which I did—and I did it in the ninth inning of the World Series. I make no apologies when I say that I am damn proud of that. Anyway, with the inning now over, Game 6 was going into extra innings knotted up 3–3, and the Red Sox dreams of winning a World Championship was still very much alive.

As I walked to the dugout, Mac tapped me on the shoulder and informed me that my night was over. He said that he was going to pinch-hit Don Baylor and that I was getting replaced by Bob Stanley. I had pitched two grueling innings (which felt like ten), threw almost forty pitches, and despite the utter chaos I faced, I only gave up one hit and one run, which was caused by my throwing error to second base. It was a wild and somewhat numbing two innings that resembled a street fight rather than a baseball game. The Red Sox were still in a good position to win, and I was going to get to watch the rest of it unfold from the dugout. I caught my breath, sat down, and decompressed at the end of the bench. Although I was not happy about giving up the run in the eighth, I was pleased with the way I had fought my way out of two very nasty situations that could have ended the game. It was time to move on to the tenth.

Evidently, the baseball gods didn't think this game was good enough because it was about to reach a whole new level. Dave Henderson, whose heroics in Game 5 of the ALCS were still reverberating through the baseball world, would strike again. Leading off the tenth inning, Dave absolutely crushed a Rick Aguilera fastball and sent it flying over the left-field wall. The dude was amazing, and we were going crazy in the dugout celebrating the lead he delivered for us. In the midst of this chaotic scene, which only mildly defines what was happening in our dugout, Mac scurried over and told me to grab a batting helmet because I was staying in the game. Ten or fifteen minutes had passed since he told me I was done, and his decision caught me completely off guard. Since I hadn't batted all season, I found myself fumbling around the chaotic dugout in search of a helmet that fit. When I finally found one, I went to the plate for my first at-bat in over a year. Again, there was no time to take it in. One minute I was sitting in the dugout completely out of the game, and in the next, I was at the plate, batting in the World Series. Very few people know that story, but it's exactly what happened. Anyway, hectic is the only word to describe that moment. Needless to say, Aguilera made me look like a child by striking me out with just three pitches, but I'm telling you, an embarrassing at-bat in front of millions of people was the furthest thing from my mind. I was going back into the game, which meant I had to deal with the adrenaline dump that had already taken place and get refocused on the task at hand.

The top of the tenth was far from over. Boggs came to the plate with two outs and ripped a double into the gap. Marty Barrett followed with a single, and we scored another run. With Shea Stadium intensity at its peak and a World Championship on the line, we had scored two runs in the top of the tenth and taken a 5–3 lead. This was an awesome display of both the resilience and the champion's spirit, which were hallmarks of our team. We were playing to win and only three outs away from getting it done.

With the World Championship on the line, in the bottom of the tenth inning, I faced Wally Backman and quickly got him down 0–2 in the count. He popped out to left on the third pitch, and we were now two outs away. Keith Hernandez came up next, and I had him down 0-1. He then fought me to 2-1 and, on the fourth pitch, flew out to center field. We were one out away from winning it all. Gary Carter came up next, and he fouled off the first pitch to go 0-1. Facing a 2-1 pitch, he got a hit to left field, giving the Mets a glimmer of hope with a runner on first. My old roommate from Jackson, Kevin Mitchell, came up next and fouled off the first pitch to go 0-1. He hit the next ball to center field for a base hit, and now, with two outs, they had runners on first and second base. Ray Knight came up next and took the first pitch for a strike. On the next pitch, he hit a slow roller down the third-base line that barely went foul, and now I was sitting on a 0-2 count. The Boston Red Sox were one strike away from winning the World Series.

Over the years, there's been a sea of discourse since this specific moment happened, but only one person knows what was going on inside of my head at the time, and that person is me. With that said, allow me to describe it for you. There were nerves, there was excitement, and there was focus to the point that I couldn't hear a thing. The whole moment boiled down to a simple, single thought. Standing on the mound with a 0-2 count, the only thought I had was to strike his ass out, and I was damn sure I could do it. Being that it was 0-2, I didn't want to give him anything too good to hit, but at the same time, I knew Ray wouldn't chase anything too far out of the strike zone. Besides, getting too fancy brings a lot of bad possibilities into play, and that wasn't going to happen here. I had thrown a lot of pitches that night, and I couldn't properly gauge the impact that had on my velocity, but I was confident that I could get a high, inside fastball by him, so that was the pitch that I chose. With Gedman fully on board and everything I had left in the tank, I let loose my fifty-fifth pitch of the game, which flew out of my hand with baseball immortality on the line. When the ball was halfway there, I knew immediately that it was traveling lower than I had planned. It was inside like I wanted and had good velocity, but it just wasn't high enough. Knight swung and got a small piece of it. I watched helplessly as this innocent-looking, lightly hit baseball carried itself over the infield and landed softly on the outfield turf of Shea Stadium. It was far from innocent—it was a hit. Batter wins. Period. End of discussion.

Baseball can be a game of inches, and the fact was, I missed that pitch. Now don't misunderstand me, it was still a tough pitch to hit, but at 0-2, he should have never seen the likes of what he got. I gave him the opportunity to make contact, and sometimes in baseball, that's all you need. As the ball fell into center field, Gary Carter rounded third and scored, shrinking the Red Sox lead to 5–4. The situation was now two outs, with runners on first and third. I had my chance and sure as hell didn't need anyone to tell me that I didn't get it done because nobody was more disgusted than I was. I chose that word carefully. I wasn't devastated or disappointed—I was absolutely disgusted! You see, I didn't inherit the two strikes, I got them, and I didn't inherit the two outs. I got those as well. I was in jams the whole damn night and had finally clawed my way into a position where I could win it and did all of that against some insanely good hitters and under the most ridiculously intense circumstances the game could offer. The fact that I lost that battle against Knight when I was in control of it, coupled with what I had gone through to get there, is something I will take to my grave. Not because the critics want me to or think I should, but because winning was all that ever mattered to me, and I didn't get it done when I had a golden opportunity to do so.

With that said, we were still one out away from winning a World Championship. Clinging to a 5–4 lead, Mac pulled me and brought in Bob Stanley, who had to face Mookie Wilson with Kevin Mitchell on third and Knight at first. Mookie fouled off the first pitch and then took two straight balls. Stanley got another strike and was sitting on a 2–2 count. Once again, we were one pitch away from the title. Mookie then faced two very good, game-ending type pitches and fouled both off to stay alive. All hell broke loose on the next pitch when Stanley threw it wide, and Gedman couldn't get to it. I'm not sure if they got their pitching signals crossed up or what happened, but all I know is that the pitch got by Gedman. Mitchell scored from third while Knight went to second.

The field was now shaking as the fans went completely out of their minds. The Mets had battled back from certain death to tie the game. With the count now full, Mookie fouled off yet another two-strike pitch to stay alive. Needless to say, this was an impressive at-bat by Wilson because Stanley had him off balance the entire time, yet Mookie kept fighting to stay in it. The next pitch and the play that would result from it would go down in history. Stanley threw a damn good pitch, and Mookie got a small piece of it which resulted in a relatively innocent ground ball heading towards Bill Buckner at first base. Bill was playing way behind the bag and came up charging to field it. Being well aware of Mookie's exceptional speed, Bill, who was slowed by ankle problems, knew that the play at first was going to be very close. As he anticipated having to beat Mookie to the bag, the ball went under his glove and between his legs, rolling helplessly into the outfield. Knight scored from second, and the game was over. Bedlam ensued, and for the forty-second time that year, the Mets had come from behind to win a game. Unlike the other forty-one, however, this one would never be forgotten.

There was no time to sit around and analyze what went wrong in Game 6 because Game 7 was the next day. As devastated as we all were, we were still in the hunt for the title. Everyone wrote us off, giving the Red Sox no chance to win Game 7. We had seen what the Angels had gone through when we did the exact same thing to them, and I think that we learned from it. Of one thing I'm certain—and it's the only thing that mattered—the guys in our locker room believed we could still win it all.

Game 7 was canceled for rain which put the finale off for a day. This was a mixed bag for us because it allowed for some rest, but it also gave us another full day to think about what had transpired on Saturday night. Either way, it was Hurst against Darling for all of the marbles. In the second inning, our bats got to Darling, and we scored three runs led by back-to-back homers from Evans and Gedman. This was huge because Bruce was pitching exceptionally well for us and winning damn near every time he took the mound. He rode this 3–0 lead all the way to the sixth, but in that inning, the Mets batters came alive, and they finally got to him. They scored three runs to tie us, which changed the whole complexion of the game. This turn of events breathed new life into Shea, and the Mets transformed themselves from prey to predator before our eyes.

I was in the bullpen with the other relievers, as was Roger Clemens, who was also throwing and getting ready. Keep in mind that this was Game 7, so all hands were on deck. After the sixth and with the game tied, Mac pulled Hurst and called on me with hopes of curtailing the wave of momentum rising from New York. There has been a lot of speculation as to why Mac chose me over Roger, but that was irrelevant to me as I went to the mound. The first batter I would face was none other than Ray Knight, and it was apparent from the onset that the Mets fans weren't going to let me forget about Saturday night. They do that better than any fans in baseball. At this moment, I had become the sole focus of their infamous wrath, and as Knight stepped into the batter's box, a stadium-wide chant of C A L V I N ... C A L V I N broke out and echoed throughout Shea. I'd like to tell you that I just ignored it, but it was so thunderous and totally in sync that it was impossible to ignore. In a way, it was really cool, and in another way, it really wasn't. I can honestly say that this was a first for me, and dealing with it, as well as the Mets' tsunami of momentum, was sure to be a major challenge. I got an early strike on Ray, which helped settle that shit down a bit, but two consecutive balls brought the thunderous chant right back to the decibel level it was at before.

On a 2–1 pitch, I threw a fastball that Knight crushed, sending it out of the park for a leadoff home run. It was the first home run I had given up since August and a disastrous time to end the streak. In the battle between Ray and me in Game 6, I was in control of that at-bat even though he would ultimately win it. This time, he just kicked my ass, and I'm not too proud to admit that it was unsettling. These types of situations (the ones that had defined my last four innings) can eventually beat a pitcher down, and Ray's blast sent me to the canvas. A strikeout, pop-out, or even a simple base hit would have been enough to get me acclimated to the brutal situation surrounding me, but a driving home run on the heels of what I had experienced forty-eight hours earlier was damaging. At this juncture, I would love nothing more than to tell you about the third redemption story of my life, but unfortunately for me, there was no redemption in Game 7 at Shea. After the blast by Knight, I had to pull myself off the floor, which I did, and was again ready to fight through the inning and mitigate the damage. I had done this many times before in my career and had every confidence I could do it again. This fight, however, would end abruptly when both Dykstra and Strawberry got hits which brought Mac to the mound and sent me out of the game. Three runs were scored in the seventh, two while I was in and one after I left, and all would belong to me. The score was now 6–3.

Thankfully, it wasn't over yet. Behind some clutch hitting, we made a damn nice comeback in the top of the eighth. Buckner and Rice led off with singles, and both would score when Dwight Evans blasted a double that went to the right center field wall. With Evans on second and no outs, it appeared that we were not only going to tie the game but may actually take the lead again. Our next batter, Rich Gedman, absolutely smashed a line drive, and for a brief second, there was real cause for concern for the crowd at Shea. Unfortunately, the shot hit by Gedman went straight to the second baseman for the first out of the inning. Pitcher wins. The Mets eventually got out of this jam and limited the damage by keeping Evans, the tying run, stranded on second. We were now back in it and down by only one run, 6–5. Unfortunately for us, their red hot bats never cooled down, and in the bottom of the eighth, they blew it wide open by putting two more on the scoreboard. The Mets had scored a total of eight runs in their last three innings. As sickening as this was, they deserve credit for the clutch hitting that produced so many runs. The fact that they accomplished this in the final three innings of the World Series is more noteworthy. In the end, this onslaught of blows was enough to put us down for good. They closed us out in the ninth, and it was all over. The Red Sox had made one helluva run and played some exceptional baseball throughout the year, but in the end, the World Championship would have to wait a few more years before it came back to Boston. As for New York, Ray Knight was named MVP of the Series, and the 1986 Mets successfully secured their place in baseball history.

After the game, I walked to our locker room, got out of my uniform, and sat down. Reporters were everywhere, and of course, they wanted to talk to me. Although I was in a fog, I answered their questions as best I could, but the devastation I felt in my heart was difficult to deal with. When the interviews ended, I hit the shower and packed up to leave. On my way out, I stopped by the opposing locker room to congratulate the guys I knew from my time with the Mets. I talked to Ron Darling and Keith Hernandez, as well as my old roommates from the minors. Although it was hard as hell to be in there, I felt it appropriate to acknowledge their achievement, and they demonstrated nothing but class in return. Battered and numb from what had transpired in the previous forty-eight hours, I eventually made my way to the exit gates of Shea Stadium. I stood there alone, staring into the New York Night, trying my best to make sense of it all. I then quietly exited the stadium, oblivious to the fact that the world I was about to enter was much different than anything I'd ever known.

· · ·

The Series had broken boundaries on multiple levels. It has been estimated that Game 6 drew an audience of close to forty million and that Game 7 shattered the World Series record by drawing over fifty-five million. The 1986 World Series is still regarded in the top five of all time, and as far as Game 6 was concerned, it would go down as one of the greatest baseball games ever played. You would think that the raw, dogged passion and unyielding desire to win that defined this epic clash between the '86 Pennant winners would have been enough to satisfy even the harshest critic, but you'd be wrong. At the time, I was twenty-four years old and thought that getting to be a part of this was one of the great blessings of my life. However, for a few others and me, it soon became an inescapable nightmare. In the days and years that followed, Bill Buckner would get ruthlessly hammered, as would McNamara, as would Stanley, as would I, and there wasn't a damn thing any of us could do to stop it.

Striking out Danny Heep to save Game 1 of the 1986 World Series at Shea Stadium. Bruce Hurst threw a real gem that evening. Below, celebrating the Game 1 victory. Bruce and I are in the middle the group.

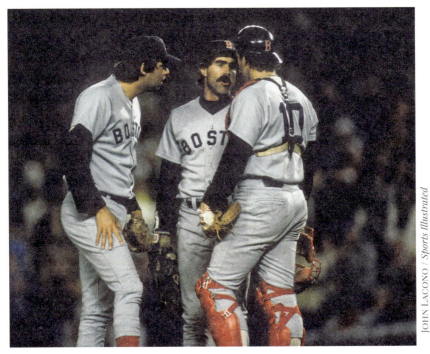

Bill Buckner, Rich Gedman and me, meet on the mound in the eighth inning of Game 6, after Lee Mazzilli reached first base on a grounder through the infield.

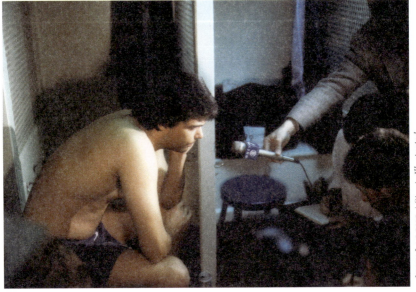

Talking to reporters after Game 7 of the 1986 World Series. My world would never be the same.

Chapter 10

AFTERMATH

There is only one way to avoid criticism: do nothing, say nothing, and be nothing. —ARISTOTLE

IN THE DAYS FOLLOWING the World Series, I was still numb and trying my best to come down from what had just transpired. To wake up and find myself in a dark place was nothing new for me, and I remember doing what I had always done—internalize it all, figure out what I'd done wrong, and try to come back stronger. Because this had all unfolded on one of the biggest stages in sports, and coupled with the fact that a World Championship was lost, I was aware of what lay ahead and that it would be tougher than anything I had ever faced. You see, in my mind, it didn't come down to Buckner or any decision that Mac made. It came down to Game 6 and a single moment in time where I had a batter down 0-2 and didn't get him out. Throughout my baseball life, I relished moments like those, and rarely ever had I let someone escape such a situation with the game on the line. In fact, during the 1986 season, I didn't give up a single hit when I had a batter down 0-2. Not once. That's why this particular moment was consuming me. These are the types of struggles that take place far away from the bright lights and cameras. They are also what make playing professional sports so difficult. One minute, you're in front of millions of people playing for the ultimate prize, and the next, you're alone in the dead of night, staring at the ceiling in search of answers that may never come. It can be a haunting existence because there are no guides or books that can help you get through it. It's just something you have to figure out on your own. Although I was very down on myself, I was confident I could find my way through it as I had done so many times before. The way I saw it, I'd have this all worked out by spring training, and then I would move on with my career putting the whole experience behind me. My goal was as ambitious as it was ignorant and would turn out to be the most naïve bit of thinking to ever cross my mind. Simply put, the ferocity of the storm awaiting me was completely undetected, but that would all change very soon.

We arrived back in Boston, and soon afterward, the city held a street parade in honor of their beloved Red Sox. I had mixed feelings about attending the event, mainly because my nerves were still raw, and I wasn't quite sure how we'd be received. My thinking was that if the fans perceived me the way that I perceived myself, it could end up being humiliating, and I didn't want Deb to see that. Boston fans are passionate, so passionate that they adore you when you are playing well and will let you know when you're not. Bob Stanley is a good example of this. Bob had signed a huge contract a year earlier, and with that contract came big expectations. When those expectations weren't met, they let him hear about it. Many times during our '86 run, Bob got booed at Fenway, which was hard as hell to watch. With that image in my mind, they loaded the team and our families on flatbed trailers, and we were driven slowly through the streets of Boston en route to a reception at City Hall. My biggest fear was that the fans would set their sights on me, and with nowhere to hide, I would be publicly shamed with Deb at my side. Those fears, and the anxiety that accompanied them, were real and should give some insight into just how scrambled my thoughts had become in the days following the World Series.

As it turned out, the mind can be a dangerous place because nothing in the world could have prepared me for what that trailer ride was really like. A sea of people lined the narrow streets of the city, enthusiastically cheering us as if we had won the crown. The crowd was estimated to be 750,000, and there wasn't a hint of negativity as we were paraded through Boston. When we arrived at City Hall, the crowd awaiting us was massive, with everyone cheering at the top of their lungs and waving signs that showed nothing but appreciation for the team. We unloaded from the trailers and made our way to the stage where both the mayor and Red Sox radio announcer addressed the crowd. The scene was so electrifying that it's safe to say that none of us had ever experienced anything close to it. One by one, the players were introduced, and when they announced Bill Buckner, the streets erupted in cheers. It was such a wonderful moment and had to be meaningful to Bill as he stepped forward and tipped his cap.

A few players later, they announced "Calvin Schiraldi," and the same thing happened—the fans erupted in cheers. It was incredibly heartfelt and extremely emotional for me as I stepped forward and waved to the cheering sea of Red Sox fans. In my mind, this assured me that they appreciated the grind I had been through in those last two games, and more importantly, recognized my play throughout the season. It was such a class move, beyond comprehension, really, and it lifted my spirits at a time when I needed it most. I'll never forget their gracious show of support. What's more, at the time, I believed it would do wonders in helping me get through the off-season, preparing for 1987, and working through all the negative thoughts in my mind.

My personal thoughts aside, think about the fact that 750,000 people showed up to greet the losing team of the World Series. I challenge anyone to find another time in sports history when something of that magnitude happened. The celebration was deeply appreciated, and none of us will ever forget.

Within days of the parade, reality took over. After the dust had settled and the off-season began, it became apparent that the events of the series weren't going to fade away anytime soon. The fans had made a pretty emphatic statement of how they felt at the parade, but sports media wasn't ready to move on yet, not even close. They immediately went after Bob Stanley, who was already one of their established targets, and then they set their sights on McNamara, Bill Buckner, and me. Here's how it went. The media were not happy with the amount of money Bob had received in his contract as compared to his play on the field, and they packaged this up neatly and magnified his performance during the Mookie Wilson at-bat. They highlighted the "wild" pitch, as well as the fact that Bob didn't get him out despite having several two-strike pitches to do so. Of course, they gave no recognition to Mookie (who was outstanding during that matchup) or the quality pitches that Stanley threw because that didn't fit the narrative. They then turned to McNamara on several fronts, starting with the pulling of Roger from Game 6, which they didn't like at all, and then for not letting Don Baylor pinch hit for Roger after Clemens' departure.

Next, they nailed him for keeping an injured Buckner on the field and keeping me in the game in the tenth inning. They also blasted Mac for making the decision to put me in Game 7 when Roger was in the bullpen and available after Hurst left. I knew it was just a matter of time before they made their way to me, and I was right. I got blasted for giving up the base hits and not getting Knight out with a 0-2 count. "How stupid could he be to throw a pitch that Knight could hit when sitting on a 0-2 count?" was a predominant theme and just a small sample of what many comments were like. As unpleasant as all of this was, nothing compared to what they unleashed on Bill Buckner. Listen, I fully understand that a routine ground ball getting by a Major League ballplayer in the World Series is news and provides networks with good footage for their audience. But what happened to Bill went way beyond that, and the media were hellbent to ensure he never forgot it. The saddest part about this is that Bill was the ultimate Red Sox who gave everything he had and then some to bring that championship back to Boston. Did he (or any of us) expect a pat on the back from the media? Hell no, we didn't, but we sure as hell didn't expect to be demeaned and mocked either, and that's exactly what happened.

With the media onslaught as the backdrop and the celebration parade fading into memory, I couldn't help but think about the sad place the sports world was devolving into. Out in California, Donnie Moore had been getting pummeled from the time the ALCS ended. They afforded that man no mercy, and keep in mind; this is the same guy who took cortisone shots in his pitching shoulder just so he could play. His injuries were significant enough to put him on the sideline, but he chose to compete and be with his team. I had those shots later in my career, and I assure you that they are so painful it's hard to describe. They didn't care about any of that, and in the end, his reward for daring to re-enter the arena would be a ruthless mocking and the label of "choker" permanently tattooed on his legacy. Did Dave Henderson or any of the Red Sox label him this way? Hell no, they didn't. Sportswriters, baseball talking heads, and some Angel fans, most of whom never played the game, tattooed this on him, and it was so bad that Donnie never recovered from it.

In the northeast, the same playbook was used. One of the greatest World Series in history was being marginalized before our eyes, and in many ways, so was the game of baseball. It became clear to me that the prominence of the series was not going to stand on its own merits and that somebody, somewhere, was going to be the scapegoat. That die had been cast well before the series ended with writers ready to pounce on how one team lost rather than how the other team won. Let me explain what I am saying here. Had Boston won, and I think it's pretty obvious that we could have, the media would have gone after the Mets players in the exact same way they came after Donnie Moore and the way they came after us. I'm absolutely certain of that. Although the "collapse" of Red Sox pitching was a favorite talking point and we were labeled "chokers", the Mets' pitching, in the final two games of the World Series, gave up twenty-two hits and three home runs. Trust me, had they lost that wouldn't have gone unnoticed. Ray Knight was being teed up for the error he made in the seventh inning, which, late in the game, had cost the Mets the lead. Rick Aguilera also gave up the lead and got hit hard by the Red Sox, so he certainly would have heard about that. Ron Darling gave up back-to-back home runs early on in Game 7, and with Hurst on the mound for us, it could have proved fatal and would have been a narrative for sure. Davey Johnson would have been tarred and feathered for not bunting Howard Johnson with runners on first and second with no outs, not to mention a few other things. Davey actually gave the Mets a day off after we won the first two games in New York. This was later heralded as a genius move but had they lost, I doubt the word "genius" would have been used.

There were plenty more imperfections that would have been molded to fit the narrative of their choosing. This was all disturbing to me and represented the sad and pitiful truth about all of it. Instead of appreciating what it took to win this epic series, the final outcome was going to be reduced to somebody "choking" or somebody "screwing up," which completely dismisses the other side of the equation. It shows no respect for the Mets comeback or the classic seven-game duel fought by these two incredible teams. Most importantly, it shows no respect toward the game of baseball.

These were battle-tested and accomplished pennant winners who also happened to be, in 1986, the two best teams in baseball, locked in an epic dogfight for the ultimate prize. One of them had to lose. Both teams were laden with hardened players, not to mention several Hall of Famers, who gave everything they had in an all-out attempt to bring the coveted trophy back home to their fans. It was a beautiful and rare display of the will to win, taking place on the biggest stage, but in the end, it was all reduced to finding a scapegoat.

To me, none of it made sense. I didn't close Knight out despite having a 0-2 count, and nobody understood that better than I did, but to have some beat writer who has never played baseball say things like "He choked," or that "He was overwhelmed by the stage," was total bullshit. To have them demean Bill by mocking him over and over for choking on a simple ground ball, giving no regard to the complexities of the play, was bullshit as well. If all of this sounds like I'm trying to deflect attention from my performance, rest assured, it is not. Nobody was harder on me than I was on myself, and that's because I'm a competitor.

Again, make no mistake, I'm not hard on myself because some sportswriter thinks I should be. I'm hard on myself because my only objective was to win, and I didn't do it when I had the chance. Coming after me, Bill, or anyone for that matter, may have been the easy thing to do, but it had a belittling effect on a monumental series and ultimately discounted what the Mets were able to accomplish, or the Red Sox had we won. Regardless of how I felt, this is the way it was and how it was going to be, and there was no putting a stop to it. Any word that came out of our mouths would be seen as an excuse, and in the world of professional sports, that's simply not allowed. In other words, we were defenseless against any and all attacks and became the proverbial targets for anyone wishing to take their shot. It was confusing, and I didn't understand any of it, but then again, I was still young and very naïve.

The 1987 season finally arrived and began in the worst way imaginable. We were swept by the Brewers in a three-game series in Milwaukee. We headed back to Boston for a series against the Blue Jays, our first games at Fenway since the World Series. The fans were still hopeful about what 1987 might bring, so when Bill Buckner stepped to the plate for the first time, the crowd gave him a rousing ovation as if to say, "All is forgotten, and let's do it again this year." The reason for the Red Sox fans' optimism was the 1986 roster was still virtually intact. Everyone, including the players, had their sights set on getting back to the World Series. This optimism, however, began to fade as we hovered around .500 through April and May.

I started the '87 season by getting saves in my first two outings, and early on, I felt very good. As the season progressed, the mood around Boston began to change, and by June, it began to deteriorate. I wasn't pitching poorly by any stretch, but for the fans, anything other than a save or a win was clearly taken to heart. Again, these people are passionate about the Red Sox, and it was becoming apparent that the magic displayed in 1986 did not transfer to 1987.

They soon became restless, and as we gave them less and less to cheer about, the fans turned their focus back to 1986 and what could have been. Keep in mind, this wasn't hard to do because the media never let it go. The past gave the fans something to grab on to as the present season was slipping away. I remember losing a save in Fenway during this time and getting my first taste of what it was going to be like. As I left the mound, I was booed, and I don't give a shit how tough you think you are, it sucked. From that point on, either I won, or I got booed. It was worse for Bill. If he made an error, the next time he came to the plate, a chorus of boos would echo throughout Fenway Park. The class, the support, and the dignity demonstrated months before now dissolved into a distant memory. Bill Buckner was going to pay openly for that Game 6 error. All in all, it was really just frustration manifesting itself because of the '87 team's lack of success, but it unfairly came down on Bill harder than anyone. For the next month, he faced this sad scene, which was very hard to watch because we all loved Bill and knew what a hardened competitor he was.

Playing on the road was brutal, and it would be so for the rest of my career. Whether I was in the bullpen or coming to the mound, the heckling was relentless and targeted me personally. Opposing fans would say things like, "Hey Schiraldi, aren't you the dumb ass that cost your team the World Series?" "Glad you're going in Schiraldi, we now have a chance to win." "Hey asshole, why do they even let you play? You're the biggest choke in the history of baseball." "Hey 31, you were one strike away and nutted, ha-ha, you suck!" For the sake of this book, I only repeated the nice stuff. Most of what I heard is unprintable. To watch a kid yelling, "You suck, Schiraldi" as his father stood by laughing was much harder to take than some drunk hurling insults at me. I can tell you I wasn't ready for any of this, and it was very difficult to wrap my mind around it. I do recall how good it felt to shut them up by beating their team, but that was only short-lived because even then, they would harass me as I came off the field with shit like, "Big deal, you won a meaningless game. We all know you can't win the big one."

As bad as it was, losing under these circumstances was simply merciless. Everything was magnified and much more difficult than it would have otherwise been. From the time I was a child, losing always bothered me, but now I'd have to walk off the field to some jackass yelling, "You're pitiful, Schiraldi!" or "You're the worst pitcher ever—you suck." Just one year earlier, I had finally reached the Majors and had my whole career ahead of me. Now I was facing this shit every time I took the mound, and I can assure you, it was a dark and lonely existence. This was the aftermath I had created by missing that pitch in front of forty million people, and if I didn't figure out how to navigate it all, it could ruin my career and possibly wreck my life. That's how bad it was.

Deb was incredible during this time, but I never brought any of this home to her. We had a great relationship and lived a normal, happy life doing all the things that young couples do, but she was unaware of how hard I was taking it all. I had put up a facade, refusing to let her in because I was hell-bent on not bringing work home with me. It's exactly how my father was, and it was the only way I knew. The dangerous downside to this was that I was getting crushed from within, and I didn't know where to turn. As the pain became unbearable, I finally found a way to make it go away long enough to keep my sanity—drinking. Remember, my father spent his weekends at the bar and was a heavy drinker himself, so I am not suggesting that I discovered drinking at this time. What I am suggesting is that my drinking went from social to therapeutic and that I found alcohol to be a great escape from the world I was facing. I discovered my own way of coping, and to me, that's all I needed to keep my journey going.

A few weeks after the All-Star break, the Red Sox had a losing record of 48–54 and were sitting a distant fifth in the East Division, fourteen games back of the Detroit Tigers. Roger was on his way to another twenty-win season, and Boggs, Evans, and Greenwell were all hitting the cover off the ball, but other than that, the team was average at best. It was apparent that a repeat of the 1986 season was not going to happen, and the more this became obvious, the more the fans would let us know it. The booing of Bill Buckner, which had begun a couple of months earlier, had gotten even worse. Bill was a warrior and one of the true gentlemen I have ever known. Before and after every game, he'd have multiple ice packs on different parts of his body just to get through it. He was a man's man and the epitome of what a competitor is, not to mention he was still one hell of a ballplayer. These were hard times on him, but he never quit. He answered the call every time he was asked to do so and did it with a body that was broken and a reputation that had been willfully and shamelessly tarnished. On July 24, Bill Buckner was released by the Boston Red Sox and would never have to hear another boo at Fenway Park. It was sad as hell to watch his incredible Red Sox career end the way it did, and we all knew there was something fundamentally wrong with the way it happened.

The season continued on for me, but nothing would really change. If I didn't do well at home, I was booed, and no matter what I did on the road, I was heckled. There were times when I preferred to pitch away from Fenway because I just didn't want to hear it anymore; it was that hard to take. I ended up having a decent year (8-5 with six saves, a 4.41 ERA, and ninety-five strikeouts), but I could never have imagined seeing or experiencing the things I did that season.

One thing was certain, I was no longer naïve about any of it, and I knew exactly what to expect from that point forward. The mocking and shame had opened my eyes to the ugly side of professional baseball, but I wasn't about to let this ruin my love for the game or my passion for competing. What lay ahead was just another challenge with greater obstacles but the same prize, and I wasn't done trying to fulfill my dream just yet.

After the season ended, I received notice from the front office that I had been traded to the Chicago Cubs. I was only in Boston a little over a year, but I learned so much, and I left there a better player. Despite everything that happened, I enjoyed Boston and appreciated their fans because we had two things in common. First, we both believed that the game of baseball was special and worthy of passion. Secondly, we believed that winning meant something and should always be the goal.

I have to admit that I didn't like their treatment of me in '87, but in a sense, I understood it. Before I threw that pitch, I held a lot of dreams in my right hand on that October evening at Shea, and I certainly played a role in those dreams getting crushed. I just wished that they could have understood that those were my dreams too and that I gave everything I had to get it done. It didn't need to get personal, and it sure as hell didn't need to go to places like "He was scared to be out there" or "The stage was too big for him." Not only was that completely false, it demeaned me as an athlete. I wished they had understood that.

I also wished that they could have seen what I was going through on the road while representing the Red Sox as best I could, only to return back home to Fenway and get booed by our own fans. I'm not convinced they would have done that had they known what some of us were enduring at the time. With that said, I also understood that the true Red Sox fans were not represented by some of the talk show hosts, writers, or the few thousand people who took it upon themselves to boo their own players.

• • •

When I think of Red Sox fans, my memory will be the parade where a sea of cheering people took time out of their busy schedules and welcomed us home after the most bitter defeat imaginable. As I packed my bags and headed toward Chicago's Wrigley Field, this was the memory I took with me. I gave Boston everything I had and wished more than anyone that I could have pulled it off for them in Game 6, but it didn't happen, and I'd have to live with it. It was time to move on, but I would forever be grateful to the Red Sox for giving me the opportunity to do something special, and I'll cherish fond memories of my days spent there for the rest of my life.

Chapter 11

THE WINDY CITY

New beginnings are often disguised as painful endings.
—LAO TZU

WHEN DEB AND I moved to Chicago, we were excited about the change of scenery. I was getting a fresh start with a new team, but even better, I was going to be a starter again, and in my mind, that's what my game was built to do. Boston traded both Al Nipper and me for Lee Smith, a Cubs closer. Although Lee was in the later stages of his career, he was still one of the best closers in all of baseball. This time, I didn't worry about whether or not people thought this was a good trade. I'd wasted way too much time in the past being concerned about shit like that, and all that mattered to me was getting ready for the season and working on the things I could control.

I remember my initial tour of Wrigley Field and how special the place felt. I was now twenty-five years old, and the three ballparks that I had called home were Shea, Fenway, and now Wrigley. Its history was incredible, and seeing Wrigley Field for the first time was awe-inspiring. The Cubs had one of the most loyal fan bases in all of sports, despite the fact they hadn't won anything in a very long time. In fact, it had been forty-three years since they won their last pennant and eighty years since they had won the World Series. That didn't seem to matter to the fans, though, because they showed up every season believing that this time, it was going to be their year. I felt comfortable in Chicago, discovering an inner peace I hadn't felt in over a year, and going into the 1988 season, I looked forward to it all, especially my new role as a starting pitcher.

For someone who doesn't understand the game of baseball, there's little to no difference between being a starter or a reliever. To them, the argument would be that you are pitching a baseball, so does it really matter what part of the game in which you do it? The answer is yes; it does matter, and there is a sizable difference between the two. Think of it in terms of track, where the starting pitcher is like a miler, and the closer is like a sprinter. Rarely in track will you find someone who can do both at a highly competitive level. The same is true in baseball. The starter almost always knows when he is going to play and, therefore, can prepare mentally and physically.

On the flip side, the closer can be called upon anytime, so he must be ready all of the time. The starter has at least four days to get over a bad outing or to celebrate a good one, whereas the closer has to get over a bad or good night by the next day. What's more, the closer is regularly called upon in the most precarious of situations and, more often than not, inherits stressful innings before he throws his first pitch. The starter must manage himself with the long run in mind and has to find a stride or groove as the game progresses. He also must face the beginnings of a new game, which is a challenge of its own.

Finally, rarely does a closer have to go more than one or two innings, whereas a starter can be expected to go all nine. Trust me, physically and mentally, the roles are two totally different animals, and the mindset required to do them is completely contrary to one another. Having spent the past two seasons as a closer meant that I would have to adjust everything in my mind and body for my new starting role. My advantage was that I had been a starter for most of my life, so I had plenty of experience to draw upon. My disadvantage was that I hadn't done it in almost two years, but with the off-season and spring training to prepare, I knew that I had ample time to reprogram myself.

Deb really enjoyed the sights and sounds of Chicago, often riding her bike along Lake Shore Drive. We spent a lot of time together and loved going to restaurants in the city. The last season had been hard on both of us, and it appeared that this change of scenery would wipe everything away and let us start anew. That would not be the case, however, because the events of 1986 ultimately made their way to Chicago, where it became clear that none of it was going to go away. All it took was a discussion about the Lee Smith trade, then my name would come up, and the field day would begin. Don't get me wrong, the people of Chicago were great and made us feel very much at home. It was the talk shows, print media, and radio personalities all over the country who simply could not let it go. Neither would the nut job fans who would get your phone number or send harassing letters.

It was all like a sophisticated form of bullying one would never think could happen among adults. I understand; it's kind of laughable to suggest that a guy 6′5″ and 220 pounds is getting bullied, but in essence, that's exactly how it was. When you think about the nature of a bully, what I am saying makes more sense. The bully scours the schoolyard seeking out those who have no defense and are either unwilling or unable to fight back. This is what emboldens them because they can prey on their victim without the risk of consequences because they know there's no possibility of retribution. They set the narrative for their victim by shaming them as useless, fat, weak, or scared, and when those descriptions gain traction, others join in. The bully cares nothing about the dignity of their victim; all they know is that they can do or say whatever they want at the expense of another—and get away with it. That had been my world for the past year and although I get that there is always going to be some form of this in sports, what happened to me was over the top.

Nasty phone calls, threats, articles questioning my mental toughness, the relentless mocking on the field, and talk show hosts spewing absurd things were all fair game where I was concerned.

So, what was my remedy for all this? During a game, should I storm into the crowd and confront the fans, or perhaps I should call out the writers and give them even more reason to sit behind their desks and blast me with their words? I simply had no way to defend myself, especially against the media, so they set the narrative about me without having a clue of what the experience was like that October evening in Shea Stadium. They cared nothing about what it took to get out of the jam in the ninth inning with the game on the line. In fact, that was never even mentioned. They knew nothing about how difficult it was to be completely out of the game, only to have to gather myself back together, as I was told to go back in in the tenth. They cared nothing about the fight that it took to get the two outs and two strikes or the toll that fifty-five pitches had on me during the three stressful innings I was in there.

Most telling, they conveniently forgot the save in Game 1, which took place under the same brutal circumstances but with decidedly different results. None of this fit their narrative, so they ignored it at my expense. Think about it. It's ridiculous to paint someone as scared or overwhelmed while considering the entirety of what had happened. The fact is, they wanted a choker or a whipping boy, and ignoring all of the other aspects of the series was a convenient way to create one. The results had a chilling effect that would follow me for the rest of my career and beyond, and there was no escaping it. Actually, that's not true. Several Miller Lites would set me free for a while, but as far as a healthy or real escape, there was none. Mine was a lonely and very dark existence, and it was frustrating beyond belief. Chicago was far away from Boston and New York, which was good for me, but I was still facing this shit with the new season only a week away.

The 1988 season began in Chicago with all of the fanfare that brings in every new Cubs season. We had to open up on the road for the first eight games but did really well in that stretch, going 5–3, which led the division. When we returned to Chicago for the home opener, for the first time, I got to experience what Wrigley was all about. It's difficult to describe being at a midday game in front of fans who love their team as much as Cubs fans do. President Reagan threw out the first pitch, and we went on that day to beat the Pittsburgh Pirates and improve our record to 6–3. Both the crowd and the city were as excited as they had been in years because they thought that this might actually be the team to do it. Unfortunately, we lost eight out of the next ten games and would not sniff the division lead again that season. Despite this, the fans were absolutely wonderful to watch as the season unfolded. Sure, there may have been an occasional boo here and there, but after the game, it was all forgotten, and every new game brought a renewed enthusiasm that was both uplifting and energizing.

I was in the starting rotation, and despite losing my first two outings, I rebounded for three straight, including a win over Houston and Mike Scott near the end of May. I was sitting on a 3–2 record when the pitching schedule was released for the upcoming games, and something on that paper caught my eye. On June 2, we were scheduled to play the Mets at Shea Stadium, and I was going to be the starting pitcher. I was going back to the belly of the beast, and I looked forward to this more than you could ever know. I was finally getting the chance to fight back and do it the only way their rules would allow: on the mound. I embraced the fact that it would be unpleasant, but why wouldn't I? At that time, nearly everything surrounding my baseball existence was unpleasant, but at least on this occasion, I had a chance to do something about it. The day arrived, and the bus picked us up at the airport and drove us to Shea. Upon entering the gates, I walked to the locker room, taking in the sights of the dingy old structure from within. Thoughts of that October night came pouring back, despite my best efforts to keep them out. I had no delusions about what awaited me when I walked out to the mound that evening, understanding precisely how nasty it was going to be. I put on my uniform, surrounded by my Cubs teammates, who hadn't a clue of the storm raging inside me. I then took the field for pregame warm-ups, about an hour before start time, and got my arm loose by throwing some long toss. The early bird fans at Shea were scattered about and started in on me right away, hurling every insult imaginable.

I solved this little problem by moving far away from them and going to the middle of the field, which reduced their venom to nothing but a muffled noise. Unfortunately, as game time approached, I had to move to the bullpen for my final warm-up, where I'd be throwing with a catcher and zoning in on my pitches and velocity. This is where I really got it. The bullpen at Shea is very close to the outfield stands, and as the crowd poured into the game, the scene around me became a circus, a very nasty circus. They were screaming at me from only feet away and saying shit like, "Are you kidding me? You're actually still pitching?" "Hey Schiraldi, I thought you quit," "Calvin, you suck!", "Calvin, you cost the Red Sox a World Championship," "Hey Schiraldi, do you remember 1986? We sure do, ha, ha, you suck ass!" It was relentless and hard to ignore, but damn, did it help get me ready for that game.

I finally had my chance to shut them up, and I don't recall ever being more focused. I was pitching opposite David Cone, who was one of the best pitchers in baseball and would finish third that year in the race for the Cy Young. In the bottom of the first, my time came, and I walked out of the dugout and towards the mound. There was a lot of rumbling mixed in with some laughing and, of course, mocking. You see, the fans at Shea wanted nothing more than to witness a total collapse which would further bolster their narrative against me and make for a very fun evening at the ballpark. In the end, I gave them nothing to celebrate, especially at my expense. I pitched one of the better games of my career and held them to four hits with seven strikeouts.

I ended the seventh inning by striking out Gary Carter for the second time in a row, and I ended the ninth by striking out Keith Hernandez and Daryl Strawberry. More importantly, I held the Mets scoreless the entire nine innings I was out there. I was taken out of the game after the ninth for what would have been a complete game shutout, but unfortunately for us, Cone had thrown a gem of his own and held the Cubs scoreless as well. In the top of the tenth, we finally scored a run which would have given me the win, but they tied it in the bottom half and would ultimately win the game a couple of innings later, 2–1.

This "no decision" was a hard pill to swallow, but I left Shea a little different than I had entered it. It was great to play as well as I had, especially under the circumstances, but my critics didn't give a shit about any of it and quickly moved on. That game meant something to me, however, because only I knew how difficult it was to face off against what I had to that night. I was taking on so much more than the Mets' hitters. I was battling forces that were trying desperately to convince me that I was something I knew I was not. Hearing what I had to hear for as long as I had to hear it had caused great internal turmoil, which was beginning to move in the direction of self-doubt. I needed the chance that this night provided, and it went a long way in quieting things down in my mind. Maybe, just maybe, I could now head down the road with those things a little less amplified than they had been before.

The season continued on through the summer, and the Cubs were still at .500. I was performing about the same as the team. I finally got a win over the Mets at Shea on August 4, and I even scored a run and had an RBI in that game, which felt pretty good. On August 8, history happened, with the first night game ever played at Wrigley Field. Although I didn't play, it was really something to be in a Cubs uniform that evening. The game drew national attention, and we would eventually lose it the next day following a rain delay, but I was still proud to be part of it. My best game of the year came in late August against the Atlanta Braves, where I threw a complete game and had twelve strikeouts for a 6–1 victory. In my final two games of the year, I got a win against the Montreal Expos, and a week later, they put me in the last three innings against Pittsburgh, where I picked up a save. The '88 season was a mixed bag for sure, but I felt great being a starter again. I finished the season with a 9–13 record, a 4.31 ERA, and 140 strikeouts. It was not masterful by any stretch, but it wasn't that bad either, and I felt very good going into the '89 season.

There was an air of excitement going into the 1989 season, and I think we could all feel it. It's easy to get excited in Chicago about the upcoming season because, as I mentioned previously, the fans are perpetually optimistic despite being let down for decades. This year, however, really did have a different vibe to it, and we had the players in place to make a run at a division title. During spring training, I was informed by management that I would no longer be a starter and would be returning to a closer role. The news was devastating because I truly believed I had turned the corner and that '89 was going to be a big year. But from a management perspective, the decision made sense. The bullpen had been the Achilles heel for this team, and they thought they could bolster it by putting me back there. That may have been the reason they put me in the last three innings against Montreal at the end of the '88 season, to see if they had something to work with. Whatever the reason, I had no choice and little time to reprogram my body and mind. Again, going from starter to reliever is difficult, but if I wanted to stay around, I had to make it work.

The Cubs acquired reliever Mitch Williams in the off-season from the Texas Rangers, which would turn out to be one helluva move. We started the 1989 season by going 8–2 in our first ten games. During this stretch, I registered a win and a save with my first two appearances. Williams shot out of the gate and had six saves during this early run. The excitement surrounding our Cubs team was real and would never falter throughout the entire season. We had a two-game lead going into June, and it would remain at two with the arrival of August. Mitch Williams had thirteen saves during these two months, and that year, he was one of the best closers in baseball.

I was having mixed results and could never seem to find a groove. I blew a save against the Mets, then got a win against them in late July, but nothing was consistent. What was consistent was the exhilaration in Chicago as the dream of the playoffs appeared more real with every outing. For me, the thought of returning to the playoffs was exciting, especially considering that it would be with the Cubs and in front of these fans.

By the end of August, our lead in the division stood at two-and-a-half games. Everything I have been saying about the excitement for the playoffs was now ramped up to levels not seen in years within The Windy City. Mitch was still on fire, and with a month to go, everything appeared as though it was going to happen. Then, at the end of August and out of nowhere, I was called into the office and informed that I had been traded to the San Diego Padres. I was to catch the next flight to California because I was expected to play that week. I sat there stunned, dumbstruck and devastated. There is no other way to put it. I loved Chicago, I loved this team, but more importantly, I loved those fans. Of course, there's no questioning a decision like this because, by the time you hear about it, the deal had already been made long before. Going home and having to tell Deb was really tough, but she understood the business side of baseball as well as I did. I literally had to leave her in Chicago for a few weeks so that she could do the packing and manage the details of moving out. That's how fast it all happened.

The Chicago Cubs won the NL East division for only the second time in their history. They would ultimately lose to the San Francisco Giants in the NLCS, but the season would long be remembered by Cubs fans. It was very difficult to not be a part of it and was one of the hardest things I ever experienced as a professional athlete. I had entered the major leagues as a starter with the Mets, then went to Boston as a closer, came to Chicago as a starter, and left as a reliever. As an athlete playing professional sports, I'm going to come dangerously close to breaking a cardinal rule by saying that it is very difficult to be bounced back and forth between these two positions. I'm fully aware that this will be perceived as some lame-ass excuse, but only a few guys in the history of the majors have been able to do this, and at this point, I clearly wasn't one of them.

• • •

My situation paled in comparison to a terribly sad and significant event that occurred during the summer of 1989. On July 17, former California Angels pitcher Donnie Moore shot and wounded his wife, then turned the gun on himself, committing suicide. His life had collapsed following the 1986 ALCS, and although he pitched off and on for the next two years, he was never the same player or the same person. It's been well documented that Donnie's life became engulfed by alcohol addiction and spiraled completely out of control the year after leaving baseball.

His wife, who survived the attempt on her life, pulled no punches about any of it and, in later years, blamed Donnie's personal collapse on the brutal and callous treatment he received after giving up the home run to Dave Henderson. His death was a tragic day for the Moore family and the game of baseball; as I can tell you, we were all shocked and deeply saddened by the news. I can't write about Donnie the man or what caused his tragic end because I didn't know him personally. What I can tell you, first hand, is that Donnie Moore was one hell of a baseball player and never deserved what got laid on him after Game 5—none of it.

Chapter 12

SUNDOWN IN SAN DIEGO

*Although marred by the relentless battle and weary
from the depletion of reserves, I must carry on, for the
prize I seek demands it.* —UNKNOWN

AS FATE WOULD HAVE IT, the Padres informed me when I arrived from Chicago that I was going to be a starter. The position switch at the end of the season was a pain in the ass, but at the same time, I believed it could also be a great segue into the 1990 season. I knew the ping-pong shit of moving back and forth between reliever and starter would ultimately lead to my demise, so being in San Diego was the perfect opportunity for me to establish myself as a starter and make one final career run at the position I knew best.

I arrived in San Diego after the trade-in early in September and settled in as quickly as possible. My old teammate from Boston, Bruce Hurst, was with the Padres, so it was nice to have someone I knew when I arrived. I was put in the rotation immediately and won my first game against the Astros in Houston. In my second start, something happened that was perhaps the most exhilarating experience of my baseball life. One of the things I loved about playing in the National League was that the pitchers got to hit. I loved hitting from the time I was in high school and in the National League, pitchers actually train at hitting and attend batting practice like any other player. Every time I was at the plate, except when I was supposed to bunt, I would swing the bat with bad intentions. Of course, this meant that I struck out all the time, but that had no impact on my mindset. Nobody expected shit from the pitcher, and that's the way I swung the bat.

On September 23, we were playing the Dodgers in Los Angeles. Fernando Valenzuela was on the mound for L.A., and I was on the mound for the Padres. The game was scoreless in the fourth inning with two outs when I came to the plate with two men on. I did what I had always done and swung at anything close, and on this occasion, I timed the pitch perfectly, sending it out of the park for a three-run home run. There I was, slowly rounding the bases in front of a shocked crowd at Dodger Stadium, and there was nothing like it in the world. I now only needed 754 more of them to catch Hank Aaron, but what the hell, it was a start. That moment still brings a smile to my face, and all kidding aside, it really was as exhilarating as anything I've ever felt. I ended up holding the Dodgers to one run with five strikeouts in six innings and got my second win with the Padres. I split the final two games and closed the season, 3-1 with a 2.53 ERA in the four weeks I spent in San Diego. We never caught the division-leading Giants and the season ended with us stuck in second place in the West. It was a crazy month for me, and I was disappointed to sit at home and watch the Cubs in the playoffs, but as far as setting the stage for 1990, it couldn't have turned out better.

Deb got us moved out of Chicago, and for the off-season, I met her back at our home in Austin. As a couple, we were in a good place which became even better when we received the news that we were going to be parents. Deb was excited about being a mother, and the thought of being a father could not have made me happier. Our life outside of the crazy world of baseball was very normal and yet very special. We spent the off-season getting the room ready for the baby that would be arriving in June. Being with Deb has always been one of the great joys of my life, and I will always remember that off-season as being among our best times together.

I arrived at spring training refreshed and feeling better than I had in a long time. I realized my window to do great things in the major leagues was beginning to close, which is why the opportunity that lay before me in 1990 was the perfect situation. I had a great four weeks as a Padres starter at the end of the 1989 season, and if 1990 was going to be do-or-die for me, at least it would be with me doing what I knew best—being a starter. However, almost immediately after arriving at spring camp, I was told that I would be headed back to the bullpen. I won't sugarcoat this. I didn't understand the move and was not happy about it at all. I well understood all that "baseball is a business" bullshit, but I was growing tired of it because I knew better than anyone that the chances of surviving this ping-pong existence were next to nothing. There was little I could do except get over it and start preparing with the very little time that I had, and let me tell you … it wasn't easy.

We started the 1990 season 6-4, and during this time, I was 1-0 with a save, and all came as a reliever. By mid-July, I had pitched a lot of innings, but most of the outings would be registered as "innings pitched" because I wasn't a factor in any wins or losses. My record at the time was 2-2 with a save. It was around then that I was told that they were changing my role back again and that I was going to start the game against the Reds on July 25. I almost checked the room for a camera to see if they were playing some kind of sadistic prank on me, but they weren't, and I got ready to be a starter again.

The Reds came to town, and I started the second game of a doubleheader. The opening festivities included the introduction of television star Rosanne Barr, who was slated to sing the National Anthem. I looked at the guys in the dugout and said, "What the hell? I didn't know Rosanne could sing." We all stood to get a good look as she walked out to the microphone. As it turned out, and as many of you probably remember, Roseanne couldn't sing, and before she belted out the second line, the crowd started buzzing. By the time she got halfway through the song, the boos had started raining down, and as Roseanne concluded, grabbed her crotch, and spit (in an attempt to imitate a ballplayer) the whole stadium was abuzz like a hive full of agitated bees. I watched people bolt out of their seats and march down the stairs so they could get close enough to the TV star to voice their displeasure. There's no other way to put it—she had made a mockery of the National Anthem. Now, I seriously doubt that was her initial intention because Roseanne is a comedian after all and perhaps was just trying to be humorous. Needless to say, it didn't work, and anyway you sliced it, it wasn't funny. She walked right past me as she exited through our dugout, and I vividly recall the look on her face. It was telling, and it appeared to me that Roseanne realized she had really screwed up. The fans were completely baffled, and they booed her until she was out of sight. Had she belted out a beautiful rendition of the Anthem, it would have brought the house down, but clearly, she didn't have the vocal skills, which begs the question, who in the hell made the decision to have her do this in the first place? Anyway, it was quite a way to open things up, and now time to play ball.

I pitched six innings with five strikeouts that evening and am proud to say I closed the gap on Hammerin' Hank by hitting my second home run over the left center field wall. I got to do the unthinkable for the second time, which was to stroll around the bases during a major league baseball game. It felt just as good as the first time. We won the game, and my record was now 3-2 with a save.

As if the season couldn't get any crazier, just five days later, I was a reliever again and lost a save against the Braves to close out July. In August, they moved me back to a starting role for the next five games, and I lost every one of them. Some were close, and some were not. After that, I went back to being a reliever again, all of which would go down as innings pitched with no wins or losses.

August and September were the low points of my major league career. My brain and body were exhausted from the never-ending role changes, and my shoulder was giving me problems. As my play began to falter, the heckling on the road was as brutal as it had ever been. Four years had passed since that fateful night at Shea, but you'd have thought it happened yesterday based on the intensity of the things that were hurled at me. The only way to shut them up was by winning, but even then, it would only afford me a temporary reprieve. The end of 1990 was disastrous. I walked into August 3-3 with a save and ended the season 3-8 with a 4.41 ERA and 74 strike-outs. Nothing about that season had gone the way I'd planned, and it became apparent to me that my career was officially in dire straits.

As badly as things ended, at least I could go home to Austin and celebrate something that was far away from baseball and so much more significant. In June, Deb had given birth to our daughter Samantha who brought joy to my life like nothing I had ever known. The baseball season had kept us apart for far too many days, and now I was getting to go home and be a father. The next five months were incredible. Deb was an exceptional mother, and of course, Samantha was an exceptional child. I loved everything about being a dad, and I'm not sure I ever remember being happier than I was at that time.

As grueling as it was to be away from these two, I was a professional athlete and, come spring, had to get back to work. I literally had no idea what to expect when I arrived at spring camp in 1991. Was I going to be a starter, was I going back to the bullpen, or would I be doing both again? Well, sadly, the answer was none of the above.

When camp broke, I was informed that I had been released by the Padres and found myself temporarily unemployed. I quickly signed with the Houston Astros, who put me in Triple-A to prove myself. I was damn sure of one thing, which was that I wasn't going to go through the gauntlet again. At the time, I figured this would just be for a few weeks, and that would be okay. Weeks later, the Texas Rangers bought my contract from the Astros. I played in three games with them, lost one, got heckled in all, and then was cut. In 1992, I worked out for a scout, but the truth was, the years had taken a toll on my arm, and my baseball career was over for good. I always knew that day would inevitably come, but I must admit that I wasn't anywhere close to being prepared for it.

I had played in the big leagues, all or part of eight seasons, and it seemed like I had lived five lifetimes since I was at The University of Texas. I finished my career with thirty-two wins, twenty-one saves, a 4.41 ERA, and 471 strikeouts. I spent the majority of those years playing in the dark shadows of that missed-pitch in Game 6 of the World Series.

I was branded a choker at age twenty-four, and "Schiraldied" became a new verb used to describe anyone who couldn't get it done. It was time to move on with my life, and I knew that, but this would prove to be a traumatic undertaking. You see, I was programmed early on that winning was the only thing that mattered and that no matter what, I would find a way to eventually get there. It's all I had cared about since I was a child, and you don't just turn that off. I always believed, in the back of my mind, that I would get another shot on the biggest stage and when I did, I would find redemption one more time. I was cut by the Rangers, I missed that pitch, I got heckled in ways that no human ever should, and now I was left with no way to redeem myself or get back my name. In other words, this would all become permanently attached to me as long as I lived. I wished I had had what it took to just walk away and let it go, but I didn't, and it would cost me dearly in the years to come.

I arrived back home in Austin, where being with Deb and Samantha was good for what ailed me. I truly loved being a father and a husband, but the cold, hard fact is that I loved the Arena as well. Deb, Sam, and the Arena had defined my whole existence, and one of them was now gone forever. Deb was always gracious and supportive of me, but she had not a clue of the inner turmoil that plagued her husband because I kept it from her. I was a good father and a faithful husband, but when I closed my eyes at night, I had so many things that were unresolved that I didn't know quite how to handle it all. You just don't forget what happened in the World Series, and you don't forget some kid yelling, "You suck, Schiraldi" in front of his father. In my eyes, most people would see these things as insignificant problems, so I was never going to talk to anyone about it, and I sure as hell wasn't going to seek professional help. Tragically, my unrefined answer and the only way I knew how to deal with it all was to turn these problems over to my good friend Miller Lite.

I settled in with the fatherhood role, and during this time, we celebrated the arrival of our son, Lukas. It was incredible to have both a son and a daughter, and Deb and I couldn't have been happier than the day we brought him home. Samantha didn't know what to make of it at first, but she soon adjusted and loved to be around Lukas. I loved the little guy and to see Sam right by his side made those times unbelievably special. On the surface, I had everything a man could ask for, but there was something missing and work unfinished.

Speaking of work, I wasn't during this time because we still had plenty of money from my playing days. I loved to play golf and was pretty good at it, so I spent countless hours golfing with my friends and drinking beer. On occasion, I would come home after having a few too many but always managed to function well, do what needed to be done around the house, and play with the kids. After a while, Deb began to notice that this was becoming a pattern and would make comments like, "Don't you think you should give it a rest for a while?" I would assure her that she was overreacting, that I would be fine, and then I wouldn't give it another thought.

One gorgeous day on the golf course, I was in a great mood as we were about to get a round started. A guy I was playing with introduced me to one of his friends and said, "Steve, this is a friend of mine, Calvin Schiraldi." As we shook hands, Steve replied, "Yeah, I know you. You cost me a ton of money with that pitch in 1986." He's lucky I didn't wrap my driver around his neck. I went from being in a great mood to a very dark place in an instant. I have never been a violent person or any kind of brawler (it's just not who I am), so I was kidding about the driver. However, I was genuinely pissed off, and this guy could see it. Regardless, after knocking down an obscene amount of beer, all was good in my world, and I ended up enjoying the round.

This was probably the most difficult period of my life. I had so many friends still in the league, and it was hard as hell to watch a game knowing that I would never get to play again. Roger, Spike, and I were still very close and would occasionally play golf when they got the chance. Sam and Lukas were growing up before my eyes, and I loved every minute that we were together. I knew they deserved more from me, as did Deb, but I was in a pattern of drinking and playing golf that was too powerful a release to let go of.

One day, I came home, and Deb confronted me directly for the first time. She told me that she thought I was drinking too much, and worse, she told me that I was no longer the man she had married. I assured her that everything was fine and that she just wasn't used to me being around all of the time. I said I was okay and asked her to please understand that everything was going to be alright.

Contrary to what I told Deb, I knew in my heart that everything was not alright, and her words had a crushing effect on me. I adored her, but in my mind, Deb had no clue about what I was going through. I just kept telling myself that eventually, I would have it all worked out, and things would get back to normal. I just needed a little more time. With that said, I continued playing golf and drinking every chance I got, which was often. By the way, I always drank away from home, and if I drank at the house, I would hide it. I don't want to give the impression that our home was littered with empty beer cans, and the refrigerator was always full. Deb would never allow that, and I knew it. One day I arrived home after one of my excursions, and I noticed the look in her eyes. It was one of sadness, despair, and disappointment. Deb didn't say a word because she didn't have to. I tried to ignore it, but it wasn't easy, even with an alcohol-clouded mind. She went to work the next morning at our church and, as always, took the kids with her. I went golfing and got drunk again in the middle of the day and returned home a couple of hours before they did. As I sat down and looked at our beautiful home surrounded by pictures of my children and their mother, it all hit me. I was wasting away, and just like she had said, I was no longer the man she had married. The moment was completely overwhelming and hit so hard that I actually began to cry. I fell to my knees and asked God to help me through the horrible predicament I had gotten myself into. I was absolutely broken and desperate to escape this misery. As I laid on the living room floor like a helpless child, something came over me, and I decided that this bullshit was going to end. I vowed to do something productive with my life and to be the husband, and father Deb and my children deserved. I got to my feet and immediately called The University of Texas Office of Admissions and took the first steps to complete my college degree. I decided that I wanted to be a coach so I could teach youngsters the game of baseball. It would be a great way to give back to the game that had given me so much, as well as something meaningful to do with my life. When Deb and the kids arrived home, I proudly laid out my plan. Her reaction was restrained, but there's no doubt it provided her with some relief.

• • •

Unfortunately, this would not be the end of what was going on inside of me, but it was a damn good initial step. For the first time since I left baseball, I would wake up in the morning with both a purpose and the motivation to get it done. I hadn't experienced feeling this good in a long while and was genuinely excited to get started with the rest of my life.

Deb and me holding Lukas and Samantha. I had everything a man could ask for.

Deb and Lukas.

Lukas and Samantha growing up.

Chapter 13

IN SEARCH OF
A FUTURE

*Progress is impossible without change, and those who cannot
change their minds cannot change anything.*
—George Bernard Shaw

IN AUTUMN OF 1994, I enrolled at the University of Texas in an effort to finish the degree I began fourteen years earlier. I had left UT after my junior year, so I had earned a number of credit hours and wasn't too far from completing my requirements. In order to teach and coach in the state of Texas, I would need both a college degree and a teaching certificate, a process that would take a little under two years. In those days, Select Baseball wasn't around but had it been, I probably would have gone that route because I could have just stepped right in. My most viable option was high school coaching, and to be part of that system, I had to complete this process.

Going back to the 40 Acres was interesting, to say the least. I was thirty-two years old and had seen the world in ways most never will. As classes began, I found myself sitting in rooms filled with nineteen- and twenty-year-olds who still viewed the world from

the innocence of their youth. On several occasions in class, I recall shaking my head when someone would share their thoughts on
how the world worked. They didn't have a clue, which is both the
beauty and the curse of being so young. In no way do I intend any
disrespect towards these students. In fact, they were far more focused on their studies than I was at their age. I'm just saying that as
refreshing as their youth was, they had a lot to learn about what lay
ahead. Moments like those caused me to reflect back to when I was
their age, which made me wish I could go back in time and educate
my younger self on how the world really operates and what, in fact,
lay ahead for me. All in all, returning to school was a curious and
thought-provoking experience and also quite enjoyable.

In the spring of 1996, a friend of mine from church told me
about a private school looking for an assistant baseball coach. I had
finished my degree at UT and was six months from completing the
requirements for a teaching certificate. My ultimate goal was to take
over the Westlake baseball program, where I saw a real opportunity
for a new career. Coach Bushong had been gone for several years,
and in his absence, the program hadn't been the same. There were
rumblings regarding a possible coaching change, and I was confident I would get the position if that opportunity arose. At that moment, the part-time job at the private school seemed like the perfect
segue between me finishing my requirements and landing a job at
Westlake.

St. Michael's Academy was a small private school in the hills of
West Austin. I went there as a part-time assistant coach, and it was
a great situation for me to get acclimated to a new career. The head
coach was a great guy, but he knew very little about baseball and was
first to admit it. He had taken over the program when the previous
coach left before the season started. His abrupt exit left the whole
program in a bind, so almost immediately upon my arrival, his re-
placement relied heavily on me, and by the time the season ended,
I was basically running everything. It was also the way he wanted
it, and the players didn't seem to mind. That summer, I finished
my certification requirements, and when the Westlake job failed to

come open, St. Michael's offered me a full-time job which I accepted. It was a good situation because I had experience at the school, and even better, there was a foundation of talented young players on which to build a program.

I arrived on campus in the fall of 1996, and the setting made me so comfortable that I immediately felt at home. I was five years removed from major league baseball, and in Austin, I was remembered more for what I had done at Westlake and Texas than what I had done in Boston in 1986. What's more, I melded quickly with the other coaches at the school, making my transition easy. Admittedly, I had a lot to learn about coaching. Although my knowledge of baseball would never be an obstacle, building a team and navigating the complexities of coaching young players was entirely new to me.

Despite the fact that this was a small private school, several of their programs were perennial state contenders. Baseball wasn't one of them, but that winter, I enjoyed watching our girls' basketball team. As one who loved and understood the game of basketball, I was amazed at how far girls' sports had come since my high school days. These young ladies played wide-open, full-court basketball as a team. What's more, they played with discipline and heart, worked extremely hard in practice, were all good students, and loved their coach. Observing this made me realize the baseball program's potential, especially once I had a chance to implement the vision I had for it. As determined as I was to build a high school baseball program, I suddenly understood a much deeper and more exciting meaning to this experience. When I was forced to say goodbye to the Arena in 1992, I assumed it was forever. I foolishly convinced myself that standing on a pitcher's mound and facing down batters was the only way I could compete. What I realized now was that coaching afforded me this same opportunity. It would still be my team versus another, but now I would be playing a different role, one with far more responsibilities. As a coach, I could feel and taste competition again and finally fill the void created after retiring from baseball. I no longer saw my new job as something to do but as the perfect way to re-enter the Arena and do it all within the game of baseball. Teaching these kids how to win would be the objective, and although it was going to be a tremendous challenge, it brought me renewed energy and purpose.

Earlier, I mentioned my good relationships with the St Michael's coaches, but what I neglected to mention was how good most of them were at their craft. I was amazed at the quality of their programs, especially considering how young they were. Most, or all of them, never played in college, and yet that had no bearing on what they produced in the Arena. Sure, they understood the X's and O's, but I noted that their real key to success was the connection they had with their players. Witnessing that first hand and throughout many of the programs at the school made me realize what a vital role this connection played at the high school level. Of course, I understood what it was like to have coaches like that because I had been blessed with some myself while in high school. Now I truly understood the necessity of that role, so it became my top priority in building the baseball program.

A few weeks before practice began, one of the young, part-time coaches inquired about becoming my assistant. Mike Kane was a wet-behind-the-ears assistant in volleyball and the understudy of the girls' basketball coach. He exemplified the burning desire to win, and this characteristic endeared him to me almost immediately. Although Mike was raw, he was a sponge with every coach he talked to. He was hell-bent to learn everything he could about coaching from every possible angle. Mike would do anything you asked, talk strategy any chance he could, and was never late or missed practice. He wasn't an ass-kisser, either. The dude was on a laser-focused mission and was doing the leg work necessary to be the best coach he could be. What's more, the players loved him and loved working with him, which helped me tremendously as I strove to develop relationships with the players. I mention Mike Kane not only because he was a great assistant but because it was so refreshing to see someone that young so determined to get to the top. It was great having this kind of energy around every day, and it made my transition to coaching much easier and more rewarding.

There was no getting around the fact that there was a lot of work to do with the baseball team. Nothing was consistent, and winning was certainly not a priority. Luckily, talent really wasn't the issue. The problem was with the culture that surrounded the program. Some of the kids were serious, some weren't, and most just used it as a way to play a sport in high school. The parents were a microcosm of the program where some just wanted their kids to participate, and others wanted their kids to make it to the majors. Nothing about it was focused, and the results reflected that. The situation was polar opposite from what I knew at Westlake, where every player was passionate about winning and worked relentlessly towards that objective. Changing the baseball culture was key, and if I could succeed at that, I was certain everything else would fall into place.

Early in the season, we faced off against a cross-town rival, and this game marked the moment when it all began to change. At one point, we were winning, 9-0, but became lax, and our arch-rivals came back to beat us. No one loses a baseball game after being up 9-0, and afterward, I tried my best to explain to them how it happened and what to do next time to ensure it never happened again. We boarded the bus for the trip back to campus, and we had barely pulled out of the parking lot when I began to hear some cutting up and laughing from the back.

My face was red, and my eyes were almost crossed at the disrespect being shown towards the Arena, but I didn't say anything and continued to drive. A couple of miles down the road, nearly every player was laughing, joking, and having a great time like it was a damn party. I let it continue and forced myself to concentrate on the road because I was practically dizzy from being in the presence of these fools. It was so bad that I felt like a bus driver taking first graders to a water park. This was the culture. They simply didn't give a damn about winning, and much worse, they didn't care about losing either. I couldn't begin to reconcile this, and yet I never said a word. When we arrived at the campus, I drove past the parents waiting to pick up their little darlings and headed straight to the baseball field. One of these clueless joy riders actually (and naively) said, "Hey Coach, I think you were supposed to drop us off in the parking lot."

"Hey buddy," I replied, "I hope your parents don't have dinner plans for you because that ain't happening," I then marched the team from the bus to the field, and for the next two hours, they learned a lesson about the Arena in the form of wind sprints from one end of the field to the other. After about twenty of these, I approached the players as they gasped for air. "Hey guys," I said, "let's talk about what was so funny on the trip home." There was only silence, but I kept going. "No, guys, I'm serious. I love a good joke. Please tell me what the hell was so funny because there was nothing I found funny about what I saw today. So, please cue me in on what I missed." Pitifully, they all looked at each other, but no one answered. "I'll tell you what," I continued, "We're gonna keep going until you give me your secret of being able to laugh after a game like this." I followed that with twenty more sprints.

This went on for the next two hours. Yes, I allowed for an occasional puke break, and of course, I let them have water, but I made it clear that this was never going to happen again as long as I was around. It wasn't a punishment for losing the game, as I think that's a terrible approach to coaching kids. In fact, it does immense damage to a player's spirit, especially if he really tried. My actions were an attention grabber and a good way to highlight my team's lack of understanding regarding the art of winning. With their heads hung low and their bodies spent, the team left the field with this message burned into their fun-loving brains. To their credit, nobody quit, and no one ran to his mom to complain. From that day forward, though, this Crusader baseball team began the march toward something that none of us would ever forget.

Despite how small the school was, there were some talented players on the team. One of its pillars to build upon was a junior pitcher named Rhett Riviere. Rhett was a terrific athlete with a strong arm, and working with a pitcher like him was a whole lot of fun for me. Led by Rhett and several others, the team got on a roll and gelled nicely as the season progressed.

Winning began to mean something to them, and as we made our way to the postseason, the players pushed each other to be better. Remember, a lack of talent was not the issue, as we had plenty. The problem was understanding what it took to win, and it was finally taking hold. Watching this transition was one of the most beautiful things I have ever witnessed. The kids completely bought in, and we made it to the state tournament along with five other schools. Even though I wasn't quite sure what would happen, the boys believed that they could win it all, and I loved that. We lost an early game on Friday to the top team, Holy Cross of San Antonio, which meant we had to win three games on Saturday in order to win the championship.

Although that structure may seem odd today, it's just how it was done in the private school ranks circa 1997. We won our first game in the morning and then had to once again face Holy Cross—and we'd have to beat them twice. In a dogfight that went to the very end, we won the first game, so now the state championship game awaited us in the afternoon. Resting and waiting for the game to start allowed me some time to reflect on our team. In order to get to this point, they demonstrated such grit and heart that it inspired me beyond words. To think that this was the same group who laughed their way home after that embarrassing, early-season loss made me realize something I have never forgotten. Every team and every person has a will, a determination within them somewhere, and these guys proved it in spades. As a coach, if you're lax and cool with no expectations, you'll produce a clown show. If you mandate discipline with expectations, your players will know that you care, and you'll get heart and grit in return, which always makes winning a possibility.

The championship game was another dogfight, and it was impressive to watch the will to win demonstrated by both of these two high school teams. In the final inning, with runners in scoring position and an exhausted Rhett on the mound, we got the final out and won the first baseball state championship in school history. As all hell broke loose, I made it a point to stay in the dugout and just watch the kids let it all go as they dog-piled on top of each other at the pitcher's mound. Coach Kane didn't care what I was doing and flew out of the dugout to join in the celebration. This was, without exception, the greatest moment of my baseball life because I got to witness kids I loved, feel what it was like to win something special in the Arena. I had seen and participated in games like this on much bigger stages, but I never felt the way I did on that day.

It had been a great year in more ways than winning on the baseball field. Deb loved coming to the games with Lukas and Sam, and things were much better at home. My new job couldn't have come at a better time. I loved coaching and being around the game again. I learned a lot that year, but I also knew I had a long way to go, which made me excited about next year's team and continuing to build a culture of winning.

The following year, I received notice from The University of Texas that I had been selected for induction into the school's Hall of Fame. This was a great honor for me because I loved The University of Texas and to be part of that history was incredibly meaningful. Coach Gus had left the year before and was replaced by Augie Garrido for the 1997 season. In his final three seasons, Gus' teams were not up to the standard he had established, and neither was the team after he left. It was painful to see that storied program in such a state, and that's where I focused my acceptance speech at the ceremony. I highlighted the "winning tradition" sign above the baseball locker room entrance and suggested that in order to turn things around, everyone involved needed to take a closer look at what that message represented. In my mind, and in the minds of those who played with me, these standards were no longer being met, and I felt it appropriate to point that out. In the end, it was a special evening for Deb and me and was certainly one I will never forget. As for the Longhorn baseball team, it would take a few seasons, but Augie would eventually turn things around and bring two National Championships back to Austin.

That spring, the St. Michael's Crusaders hit the diamond with a veteran-laden team and pulled it off again. It was almost a carbon copy of the year before, with us having to win two straight against Holy Cross to win the championship. I witnessed some of the toughest performances I had ever seen and key contributions from everyone. With Rhett on the mound at game's end, we pulled off almost exactly what he had done the year before, and once again, I was blessed to witness another dogpile on the pitcher's mound. We were back-to-back State Champions, but more importantly, it now meant something to wear a Crusader baseball uniform. It was tough as hell to say goodbye to that senior class because they were so instrumental in building our program's culture of winning. This group had taught me so much, and getting to coach them so early on in my career helped set a standard for both the program and myself that lasted for the next twenty-two years. Their team picture still hangs proudly in my office today. Rhett was drafted by the Minnesota Twins in the twenty-second round of the Major League Baseball Draft and went 7–0 in the two years he was in the gauntlet. He gave up baseball after his wife's mother became ill and eventually became my assistant.

At the end of every school year, we had a tradition called the coaches retreat, where we would head to the Texas Hill Country for a long weekend to unwind from our sports' seasons. Coaching was not easy, and this trip afforded us a great way to decompress and discuss the year's experiences. One of the coaches had a brother-in-law with a ranch in Kerrville, Texas, and he and his wife allowed us full access to this beautiful place every year. We fished, played golf, and played some epic basketball games in a barn with a full indoor court.

On one of these trips, I remember sitting on the porch at dusk, just taking in the natural beauty of the ranch. There were only two of us present because everyone else was down at the lake swimming. As we sat on the porch, the conversation turned to my baseball career. This fellow coach respectfully picked my brain, wanting to know what the major league experience was like. He asked if I ever got to swing the bat in the majors, so I told him about the home run I hit off Fernando Valenzuela. He got a big kick out of that and asked if I ever hit a home run off of Nolan Ryan. I laughed and told him that no pitcher was going to do that. I explained to him that Ryan was going to let a pitcher take an honest swing, but if he thought you were swinging for the fence, he'd put the next pitch right in the middle of your back. My friend thought that was one of the funniest things he ever heard and almost fell out of his chair from laughing so hard.

The conversation ultimately made its way to 1986, marking the first time I had spoken of it since it happened. It had been nearly thirteen years since that night in Shea, and it felt good to finally open up about it some. He just listened as I tried to explain what the whole experience was like. The funny thing was, most of my friends in Texas had no idea about the aftermath I faced following the series. They just knew that I pitched for Texas and played in the World Series, and to them, it didn't get any better than that. That evening, I spared him anything regarding the aftermath and let the innocence of the conversation carry on. Although it was somewhat of a relief to do this, it also made me realize that there was a lot of painful baggage I was still carrying. I had packed it all deep inside, but it was still there, stored neatly in the depths of my mind. After a long conversation about my playing days, the coach expressed to me how rare it was for someone to accomplish the things that I had, but to be honest, I never let those words take hold. I thanked him for the kind thoughts, but in my mind, he just didn't get it.

I was still holding on to not winning in 1986, and worse, I was holding on to the aftermath and the degrading things that were said about me. It's pretty sad, but that's how my mind was working, and there was no getting around it. There was a great irony at work here because, as a coach, I simply wouldn't tolerate my players holding on to something negative. I was intolerant of that because I knew it would stymie future growth and hinder their ability to move forward. In other words, I was acutely aware of the destructive nature of holding on to such things, and yet I chose not to follow the guidance I gave my own players. Again, I felt it would eventually clear up, but the fact that so much time had passed, and it hadn't, was the red flag I refused to see.

As the years came and went, I still enjoyed being a coach and maintaining all of the school's sports fields. By 2004, we hadn't won any more state championships, but we had made it to the playoffs every year and gotten really close a couple of times. Far away, the Boston Red Sox had an amazing run and made it back to the World Series for the first time since 1986. They were down 0-3 to the New York Yankees in the ALCS and, remarkably, fought back to win it. It was the only time in the history of baseball that a team had come back from 0-3 in the postseason. This was the famous "bloody sock" series where Red Sox Pitcher Curt Schilling displayed one of the gutsiest playoff performances ever seen. It was all very exciting, but having Boston back in the series was a mixed bag for me because, although I very much wanted to see them finally get their prize, I knew that my past would be dredged up and that the negative spotlight would once again be coming my way. I wasn't mistaken. Highlights of the ball going through Buckner's legs, Knight getting his base hit off of me, and Stanley's wild pitch were broadcast everywhere. "The Curse of the Bambino" was a major theme, putting many of us right back on center stage. This was all pretty difficult, so I drank a bunch and watched the final game of that series from my sofa. That evening, Deb looked the other way at my drinking because she knew this was tough on me, although I never discussed it with her openly. While watching this game, I saw a sign held by a Red Sox fan that read, "Bill, we forgive you," and it completely changed my whole demeanor.

Think about that for a minute. Although the sign was meant to be positive, it conveyed the exact negative connotation that had engulfed Bill since 1986. I mean, you forgive someone for knowingly and willingly doing you wrong, but Bill was guilty of neither. The mindset of the sign was that Bill needed to be forgiven and that the sign holder was gracious enough to grant it. It sent me back, and here I was again, trying to defend an "unforgivable" error that occurred eighteen years earlier. Sitting on the couch, I found myself right back in the middle of the storm, triggered by some stupid ass sign. The Red Sox won that night, bringing the trophy back to

Boston for the first time in eighty-six years. I was genuinely happy for those fans, and yes, I did feel a sense of relief that perhaps we could all finally move on. During the celebration in the locker room, with champagne baths taking place everywhere, the Fox Sports broadcast went to the post-game reporter for a live interview with pitcher Curt Schilling. Surrounded by the noise and chaos, the reporter asked him how he felt. His response? "I feel great for the fans of Boston, and I'm happy for Buckner, Stanley, and Schiraldi and all of the other great players who can now be remembered for the great players that they were." Here's a guy who was instrumental in winning a World Championship, and the first words out of his mouth were in reference to the fans and to the three of us. It was a class move in front of a national audience, and it came from someone who I had never even met. Schilling's gracious act meant a great deal to a lot of people, and it's one I will forever appreciate. The days surrounding the 2004 World Series had been difficult for me, but it ended with Boston finally getting their prize and with Schilling defending players from an era that had long since passed.

In Boston, the theme of closure would continue into the 2005 season during the opening game ceremonies at Fenway Park. On the same day they recognized their newly minted World Champions, the Red Sox had planned something very special: Bill Buckner throwing out the first pitch. In front of a packed house, the public address announcer introduced Bill and Fenway rose to their feet with a tremendous roar. The standing ovation lasted minutes as Bill walked to the mound, having to occasionally wipe tears from his eyes. In typical Bill Buckner fashion, he threw a perfect strike and walked off the field to an apologetic standing ovation which emphatically recognized him for who he was, as a man and a player. It was a dignified and classy tribute not often seen in the hardened world of professional sports, and I'll always commend the Red Sox organization and their fans for doing it.

Back in Austin, I was preparing for my eighth season with the Crusaders. By this time, the culture around the team was where I wanted it to be, and winning was firmly entrenched in every player's mind. My mother loved watching us play and rarely missed a home game. My father, on the other hand, rarely saw us play at all. I did, however, spend time with him on occasion, and he and I would go hunting, and sometimes after work, I would visit him at the bar he now owned. It was an interesting dynamic when we were together because we only spoke in general terms. He never asked about the team or offered any compliment concerning our successes. This is just who he was. After all, we never spoke a word about the World Series, nor did he ever offer me any comfort during its aftermath. As strange as it may sound, I still felt this void, despite the fact that I was now forty-three years old.

It was during the 2005 season that dad informed me he had been diagnosed with bile duct and colon cancer. He had beaten prostate cancer a few years earlier, but this time he made it clear that he was not going to endure the brutal treatments necessary for survival. My father was a proud man, and I knew just what that pride would lead to. Over the next few months, his health deteriorated badly, and although we still spent time in each other's company, there were no deep conversations or thoughts concerning the future, despite the limited time we had left together. On November 5, 2005, my father was traveling to a hunting lease to meet his lifelong friends for opening day of deer season. Before he got there, he pulled his truck over to the side of the road and took his own life. This was devastating news for all of us, and it hit my mother especially hard. My parents had a very special relationship. My father adored her, and she deeply loved him. To see the loss in my mother's eyes was very difficult for me to deal with. In fact, everything about his passing was difficult.

After a few days, I was sent by the authorities to retrieve his vehicle and other personal belongings. As I approached his truck, the situation was overwhelming. I gathered the courage to search the vehicle in the hope of finding some answers. I was looking for a note or something that he might have left for me or the family, but the search was fruitless. There was nothing to be found. My father had just checked out without saying goodbye to anyone. Part of me felt relief that he would no longer have to suffer, while part of me was left empty and confused, still looking for answers as to why he was the way he was. Regardless, those were answers I knew I'd never find. The way I see it, my father felt he had one job to do where I was concerned, and that was to turn me into a man. He did it the only way he knew how which was old school and exactly the way his dad had done for him. My father was a good and decent man, and to this day, I miss him dearly.

I handled the passing of my father the way I had handled anything that was bad, I drank. It was the pathetic truth about my life. I had everything a man could want, and yet something inside convinced me that the bad outweighed the good. Samantha was now an incredible fifteen-year-old attending school where I worked and was still my precious baby girl. Lukas was a strapping twelve-year-old, and I loved every minute I spent with him. Deb was a doting mother and wonderful in every way, but despite all of this, I couldn't stop drinking. Understand, I was not coming home stumbling drunk, and any drinking I did, was still well hidden. Also, I never drank around my players or before games, but I would find a way at the end of the day to down several beers. It was all so unnecessary because I had such a blessed life, but the cold hard truth was that over time, my coping mechanism, which I thought had worked so well, had become an addiction.

In 2007, Lukas entered high school and was going to play for me. Having both of my children with me at school was a great experience. Samantha had an edge to her and was more like me, while Lukas was a soft-spoken young man with more of the traits of his mother. He was quarterback on the football team and spent four years playing baseball for me, developing into a really good pitcher. By the time he left high school, Lukas was 6′-6″ and had one hell of a fastball. After graduation, he attended junior college before entering The University of Texas, where he became teammates with Roger Clemens' son, Kacy. Thirty years had passed since Roger and I played at Texas, and I think it was a lot of fun for the fans to see our kids playing for Augie Garrido's Longhorns. Both would have good careers at Texas, and both would be drafted. Lukas played in the minor league gauntlet for four years, got married, and eventually gave it up. He made it to Double-A, but in the end, chose a much more stable life and entered the Business School at Texas Tech University. Samantha married and became the proud mother of a beautiful daughter. My love for these two is indescribable, and being their father has always been the greatest joy of my life.

In 2011, I received a call from someone within the Red Sox organization inviting me to be part of a celebration honoring the 25th Anniversary of the 1986 team. I had a long discussion with Deb about attending the event because I'd been trying really hard to move on from it, and neither of us was sure what effect something like this would have on me. Ultimately, I decided to go, and it was great to see everyone again when I arrived in Boston. We attended a few parties and some autograph shows, but the main event was scheduled for that evening's baseball game, where the '86 team would be introduced in front of the Fenway crowd. When game time arrived, I walked out onto the field wearing the jersey that they had provided and thought to myself, "What in the hell have I just gotten myself into?" I was petrified that when they called my name, I would get booed. Please don't find that odd because these thoughts were absolutely real to me, and I could feel them throughout my body as I walked out there. For twenty-five years, thoughts like these had been festering uncontested in my mind, and none of it had ever been properly addressed.

After lining up on the field, they announced us one by one, and my anxiety was at a level I'd never felt. When Bill was introduced, they went crazy, but that was no surprise because they had made amends with him in 2005. When they finally got to me, and my name echoed throughout Fenway Park, a roar of cheers came down around me, which felt like a warm blanket. At this moment, it was difficult as hell to stay composed, but I tried my best as I waved back to the Fenway Faithful. It's impossible to describe the emotional release at that moment, but know it was as meaningful as it was healing. The weekend came to an end, and I couldn't possibly have enjoyed it more. It was now time to move on and let it all go, but that could only happen if I got through one of the last of the remaining roadblocks, which sadly had been placed there by me.

I served twenty-three years as the head baseball coach at St. Michael's Academy, and although we won fifteen district championships, went to the playoffs every year, and reached the final four many more times, we never won another state championship. I spent this time in a different kind of Arena, but it was still intense competition, and I loved every minute of it. I learned so much from the players I coached, and most importantly, I learned that the will to win is ever-present, regardless of what level you may find yourself.

I had experienced many wonderful things over the previous two decades. I watched my children grow into adults. Life doesn't offer anything better than that, and this still remains the most rewarding aspect of my life. Several things related to work were also very meaningful to me. I began and ended my journey as a high school baseball coach during this time and experienced many deeply rewarding things. It was time surrounded by the ambition and innocence of youth, and I was by my players' sides as they marched their way through those critical and developmental high school years. They were fun-loving, hardworking young men passionate about getting better in all facets of their lives, and I was blessed to be part of it. I even watched one of my players, Kyle Martin, make it all the way through the gauntlet and pitch in the major leagues. His achievements couldn't have made me prouder. I also watched those young coaches go on to bigger and better things, including Mike Kane, my bright-eyed assistant, who is now one of the top volleyball coaches in the state of Texas. Finally, I got a taste of closure from the aftermath of the '86 series thanks to some classy gestures by some people inside the world of baseball. Put it all together, and this was a special and fulfilling time in my life, and yet, there was still something fundamentally wrong.

• • •

Through all of these wonderful moments, I was still drinking, not because I was coping with something, but because I couldn't stop. I had become a functioning alcoholic, far removed from the stereotypical images of alcoholics who publicly embarrass themselves, can't hold a job, or become abusive to their families. Not me. I went to church, I didn't miss work, I loved my family, and I have never knowingly done harm to anyone. Despite these facts, I was still an alcoholic, and it was a helpless and dejected truth I couldn't escape. I was eighty pounds overweight, speeding toward an early and miserable death, but even so, I didn't seem to give a shit. What's more, despite being functional, I was nowhere near the person that Deb had married, having lived the past twenty years in a gray haze. I was also nowhere close to maximizing my potential as a husband or a father. I was growing very tired of it all but still refused to address it. Deb confronted me many times to no avail, and I had even confronted myself a time or two. None of it mattered because I was so ensnared, and the thought of changing was so daunting that I was too afraid to even attempt it.

I was miserable and knew that something had to give or it was all going to end badly. My reluctance to act came from the way my clouded mind viewed everything. You see, in order to change, I knew exactly what loomed ahead of me, which was another battle in the Arena. Based on the ferocity of my opponent, I wanted no part of it. This potential deathmatch would be waged against myself—a battle between the part of me that so desperately wanted to experience living again and the part of me that was controlled by alcohol. The latter made it very clear that I couldn't survive without it. Either I'd be leaving this Arena with my life fully restored, or I would be carried out of it dead, and I don't mean that figuratively. This is why I was so scared to attempt sobriety. I knew precisely what was at stake. In the depths of this unforgiving scenario, I finally convinced myself to accept the challenge, even though I gave it little chance of succeeding. This one would be for Deb and the kids, which was a dangerous choice because if I couldn't do it for them, it was never going to happen.

Me with the kids, I love everything about these two.

At our baseball banquet after the state championship. This kid
Rhett could really play.

That beautiful ranch in Kerrville, Texas. Every year the coaches went there to unwind. That porch was my favorite place to be.

Walking out on the field at Fenway for the 25th Anniversary of the '86 Red Sox. I've never experienced such anxiety before going out there, but in the end it couldn't have been more special.

Lukas and me at the outfield fence before a Texas baseball game. Lukas was a very good pitcher and I was extremely proud to see him play for the Longhorns.

Chapter 14

THE FIGHT OF MY LIFE

*Anyone can give up; it's the easiest thing in the world to do.
But to hold it together when everyone would expect you to
fall apart, that's true strength.* — CHRIS BRADFORD

THE MOST HONEST WAY to venture into this difficult part of my life is to begin with why. It's hard for people who don't have a drinking problem to understand those who do. They can't fathom why someone would trash their own body and mind and then risk everything important to them by making alcohol the solution to their problems. Therefore, why I started down this dangerous path is pertinent to my story. There's no disputing that I drank long before the '86 World Series aftermath, but I can tell you that it wasn't a problem. I enjoyed going out occasionally and having a few with friends, and there were times when I became intoxicated. So, it's important to make the point that I wasn't new to the drinking game, or that baseball was so traumatic it started me drinking because that's not the case. Also, understand that what I'm about to tell you in no way justifies my drinking—it just helps explain why I thought I needed to do it.

I was in the perfect storm coming out of the Series and was hit with two crushing blows that seemed to work in tandem. First was the fact that I had been an intense competitor my whole life, and not winning Game 6 turned me against myself. The same thing had happened in the 1982 College World Series when I severely injured Kevin Penner with that pitch. True competitors don't forget things like that, and it's a great internal challenge to move on. I ultimately bounced back from that night in Omaha, which served to make me stronger, and I was confident that I would do the same here. The only thing I needed was the time to work it all out.

The difference between these two scenarios was that in college, I got the chance to do it because there was no circus surrounding the event, which afforded me both the peace and time to work through it. In this case, I was hit simultaneously with another blow, which forced me to fight the internal battle of losing on two separate fronts. The second crushing blow was the narrative that arose after it was over, and this wave blindsided me. I was seasoned by this time and had developed a thick enough skin to handle the normal criticism that comes from being on the losing end of big games, so I can assure you that I wasn't expecting any pats on the back from anyone. Again, I was very hard on myself, so I completely understood the frustration aimed at me following the Series, but as I explained, what happened next went much further than frustration. They began to say I "succumbed to the pressure" or was "overwhelmed by the stage" and ratchet it up to "he was scared to be out there." The whole thing took on a life of its own. They took something factual (I lost), attached whatever they wanted to it, and that became the narrative that defined me. It demeaned me as a competitor and reduced my entire career to that of a choker. I knew in my heart this was not true and that any fair assessment of my body of work up to that point would say the same.

So now, internally, I was dealing with not only losing the game but with people, willingly and callously, destroying the entirety of my life's work in the Arena. I was never outwardly boastful about my past accomplishments, but deep inside, I took great pride in knowing that I had what it took, both mentally and physically, to win on any stage. Now, with a stroke of a pen or careless words flying through the airwaves, my life's work was being erased before my eyes, and there wasn't a damn thing I could do about it. I couldn't identify the force working against me because I couldn't understand why it was happening in the first place. My years in the Arena were being reduced to rubble, but far worse, they were attacking the essence of my competitive spirit, my greatest asset that had defined me since high school. This was the perfect storm that raged around me, and although I was unwilling to seek help, the pain had become too great to ignore. In order to manage it, I found something that worked, albeit temporary, but it was also incredibly destructive. The whole situation was so sad and so poorly handled on my part, but it's why I journeyed down this dark path to begin with. I wish I had understood things the way I do now, but the fact is, I was only twenty-four years old and didn't have a clue of how to seek shelter from the storm. In the end, I paid dearly for that shortcoming.

Drinking offered some reprieve from all of this, but there were always triggers that would throw me right back to the ground, and I used them as an excuse to drink. It could be an obnoxious fan hurling insults or a comment from a "sports expert" mocking me in some way, but there always seemed to be something. Again, I couldn't identify this force, and that lack of knowledge afforded me no protection from it. Almost everything said stuck like Velcro and was stored deep inside of my mind. Drinking dulled the sharpness of these attacks, but it was never enough. I soon discovered that it would take more and more drinking the next time around in order to stem the tide. Over the years, it got to the point where I didn't give a shit anymore and my once great savior, alcohol, began to convince me that maybe they were right. By the time my career was over, and I was years into my life after baseball, I found my competitive spirit had completely eroded, and I was no longer willing to even defend myself from within. Remember, I never defended myself publicly from all of this because it is simply not allowed unless, of course, you are willing to have them label you as the "excuse guy," which would fit nicely alongside "choker." Before then, however, I always defended myself in my own mind because I had great inner pride, but as time moved on and the drinking became more prevalent, that began to fade as well.

Two decades after the Series, a young reporter from Boston came down to Austin to do a story on me. As part of the piece, he wanted to talk to some of the coaches who worked with me at school, so I made the necessary arrangements. After the reporter left, one of the coaches asked, "Hey, what the hell is this 'Schiraldied' shit that the reporter was talking about." Like a virus sweeping in from the northeast, my peers had been exposed to a raw and unhealed wound from my past, and it was humiliating to have to explain it to them. Although to a man, they called bullshit on it, my mind wouldn't let their defense of me take hold. Simply put, I had reached a point where I wouldn't even defend myself, which was not only very sad but would also prove to be quite dangerous.

Shortly after that experience, the MLB Network did a documentary called "1986, A Postseason to Remember," and they flew me to New York as one of the guests. Sportscasters Bob Costas and Tom Verducci hosted the show, also bringing in Bruce Hurst and Mookie Wilson for interviews. The documentary focused on the entirety of the epic 1986 playoffs, and it was interesting to sit there while they played tapes of all the games. Both Costas and Verducci were seasoned pros who ran the show with the dignity of baseball as a backdrop. There were no gotcha questions or pointed jabs toward anyone. Instead, the pair just meticulously dissected the '86 postseason with enlightened analysis and requests for our insight. This experience, both fair and honest, should have had a healing effect on me, but by this time in my life, I was too far gone for it to have any effect at all. I'd been living in a haze for years, and this would just be another of many positive experiences of which alcohol would rob me and prevent the healing I desperately needed.

I was in my office a week or so after the show when an email came in from someone hell-bent on setting the record straight. It was long, detailed, cutting, and defined me as the sole reason the

Red Sox lost the World Series twenty-five years earlier. The author of the email talked about Bill Buckner and how I should be ashamed of myself for putting him through what I had, and then went on to describe me as the greatest loser who ever played baseball. This was addressed to me twenty-five years after the fact, but it didn't matter to this guy because he has written me a nasty email every year since. I don't tell you this story in search of pity. I'm only telling you this because I shouldn't be telling you this. That's the point. In any other world, you click DELETE and move on, but in my sick-ass world, I actually read the messages, which gave me the excuse I needed to drink. It wasn't until recently that I finally shared these emails with someone, yet for over a decade, I privately consumed every one of them and then consumed some beer to make them disappear.

On an afternoon in August 2014, Deb was sitting on the couch when I came through the door. The look she gave me was one I had seen a thousand times before, but this one, in particular, was much more devastating. She asked if I had been drinking, and as I stood there silently, her eyes welled up with tears. The look on her face was that of hopelessness and despair, and the pain in her eyes was more than I could handle. Broken down completely and with no answers as to why I had become the way I had, I quietly turned around and walked out of the house. It was the darkest moment in my life, and in the depths of that despair, I convinced myself that there was only one solution. Deb was the love of my life, and I was tired of hurting her. What's more, I was tired of being trapped in a world controlled by alcohol with no foreseeable means of escape.

I pulled my truck out of the driveway and set out for Kerrville, about 100 miles away, to watch the sunset on that ranch I loved so dearly. It was going to be the last sunset I would ever see. In my hopeless, alcohol-induced state, I decided that I was going to pull over on the way home and end my misery once and for all. This was not a thought—it was a plan. In my mind, there was no other solution that made sense. The depth of my despair was beyond description, and to be in the throes of a nemesis, this evil had rendered me completely helpless. On the way, as I listened to the radio, I heard a song from years ago and the words jarred me enough to pull over and think some.

As I parked on the side of the highway, a battle between good and evil raged in my mind. I desperately tried to make sense of it all. This may have lasted three minutes or three hours since I don't know how long I was there. When it finally ended, I was left completely shaken. Instead of driving to the ranch, I decided to go down the road a ways and get a hotel room for the night. I brought my closest companion with me, a case of beer, and my sadistic friend assured me we could get through this night together. I would end up spending several days in different hotels and all of it drunk. I was in the direst situation of my life, and yet, I still relied on alcohol to get me through it. The only positive thing to come from this ordeal was that I finally knew, in my heart, that I was completely out of control because it damn near cost me my life.

After days of being away, I finally called Deb and told her that I was coming home and that I would try to stop drinking from that point forward. Please know that it is with great sadness and humiliation that I share this part of my story, but the dangers of alcohol abuse have no limits. It's important for anyone reading this to understand the degree this addiction, or any chemical dependency for that matter, can take on the human soul. Looking back, I'm very fortunate to have survived.

When I returned home, Deb and I spent long and productive hours discussing everything, and we decided that I was going to join a group and begin my road to recovery. Alcoholism is a ruthless and selfish disease that exacts a toll on everyone involved. It ruins lives, ends careers, and destroys families. My wife didn't sign up for this shit when she married me, but being who she was, she would be by my side as I began the journey to recovery.

As I started down this road, I recalled a local sports radio show called "Bucky and Erin in the Morning," which I listened to everyday on my way to work. Bucky Godbolt was a former assistant football coach at UT, and I got to know him through the youth camps he ran on our campus. What stood out to me about Bucky was that on his show, he frequently spoke about his own struggles with alcohol addiction. To put it bluntly, I thought that took balls because there is no way in hell I would do that. You see, at the time, I saw alcohol addiction as a weakness, and broadcasting that to the masses was incomprehensible to me. Bucky, on the other hand, was open and honest about this aspect of his life and would often share his story with his listeners. I admired that about him, and listening to his words brought me hope as I stood at the trailhead of a journey I was not looking forward to starting.

Sheer willpower can get you through the first week or two of recovery, and I definitely had that going in. I experienced some night sweats and very weird dreams, but I didn't get the shakes or physical withdrawals, which, considering how much I drank and for how long, was a little surprising. Things started getting rough after two weeks, but I stayed the course and made it through the first month. The first things I noticed were that my sleeping patterns began to return to normal, and the bloat all over my body started to recede. The human body is amazing in the way it can rebound after being poisoned for so long. Unfortunately, I also experienced the negative side and questioned this new way of life almost every minute of every day. I made it through the second month without drinking a drop, but the pressure to sustain that seemed to grow greater as I soldiered on. I became irritable and tried to use every little thing that bothered me as an excuse to get off that ride. I had convinced myself that the group of people I was meeting with were so vastly different from me that I didn't belong there. This was nothing more than my addiction rearing its ugly head, but there was no way anyone could persuade me otherwise. I made it through month three, and although the colors were beginning to return, I was still miserable and on very shaky ground. Deb was terrific throughout this time, as were a couple of my coworkers who inquired daily about how I was doing and encouraged me to keep going.

Despite their support, on my ninety-ninth day of sobriety, it happened, something so egregious that I can't even remember what it was. It was probably the mail being delivered late or my dog knocking over his water bowl, but it happened, and I was done. To get over this life-altering event, I popped a cold one followed by eight more. Of course, I convinced myself that this was just to get through my recent trauma and that I would start anew the next day, but the next time I thought about it, six months had passed, and I was drinking as much as ever.

The way I saw it, I had learned my lesson over those ninety-nine days and was back in control of everything. This time, I would be much more refined in how I approached this problem. The way my mind was working, I could drink some again, and nobody would know. Of course, I would be reasonable about it, because after all, I knew what I was doing. Deb was aware that I had quit going to the group sessions, and she also knew that I was drinking, but I'm not sure she understood the extent of it, and I sure as hell wasn't going to be as sloppy as I had been in the past in regard to hiding it. The plan was as clever as it was pathetic, but I was convinced I could be the first person in the history of the world who could live a normal life controlled by alcohol.

The months became years, and the refinement of being a sneaky alcoholic was beginning to erode because alcohol always exposes you in the end. In 2016, I was contacted by Curt Menefee from Fox Sports, who wanted to know if he could interview me for his up-coming book, *Losing Isn't Everything.* The book was going to trace the lives of several athletes who had experienced epic defeats on the field of battle. I agreed to do it because I had never turned down a single interview request concerning this subject. Curt met me at school, and he was a great guy, exactly like his television persona suggests. We did our interview, and I told him about the whole ordeal and how it had affected both my life and my marriage. The theme of this interview was about how I had to build walls around my world to protect me from what was going on. What I didn't share with Curt was that alcohol was the general contractor who helped build those walls. I didn't discuss my addiction because, in my mind, it was too shameful to reveal. I still saw my addiction as a weakness, and knowing the subject matter of his book, I wasn't about to give another writer an excuse to portray me as weak. I never read the book, although I was told it was both good and fair, because I still didn't want to face what had happened thirty years earlier. Having read it or not, I know that the book was missing a key component of the story, which was that my life was spiraling out of control because of alcohol abuse.

In December 2018, I went hunting with some friends and brought my son with me. Lukas was on a break from minor league ball, and I was happy to have him there with me. Despite my indiscretions with drinking, Lukas rarely touched alcohol even though he was twenty-six years old. I was proud of that fact but also too ignorant to see what was really going on. My son stayed away from alcohol not because he thought it was unhealthy or wrong. He avoided it because he didn't want to be like me. Through all of my years of sneaking around with the bottle, I hadn't fooled anyone in my house, especially Lukas, and he wanted no part of becoming his father. Because I was so clever in my deceit, I foolishly assumed nobody knew, especially my family. Little did I know that they knew a helluva lot more than I thought, and in their eyes, I had fallen so far that they actually felt sorry for me. That, my friends, is not the position a father should ever be in. Alcohol had consumed my life so badly and made me so selfish, I would ignore everything just to drink. At home, I had become somewhat of a shame to be around. Keep in mind, I was always faithful to Deb and loved my children dearly, but I was a shell of a husband and a father and was too focused on drinking to see what I had become. Back at the hunting camp, and being that Lukas was a grown man, I didn't feel the need to hide my drinking from him. It was a hunting trip, and he would surely understand it as a time for me to let loose a little. Although he saw me with a beer in my hand throughout the day, he had no idea that I had probably knocked out a case during that time. Or maybe he did.

That evening, we got to bed early because we were getting up at 5:00am in order to reach the field before daylight. The next morning as we were in the living room getting ready, the other guys were sitting around the kitchen drinking coffee. Instead of having a cup, I went to the refrigerator and grabbed a cold one. When the popping sound of the can opening hit their ears, there was some head shaking mixed in with some chuckling. I looked up and saw Lukas on the other side of the room. "Really, Dad," he said, "It's five o'clock in the morning." As he managed a grin on his clearly demoralized face, I attempted to draw away attention from the moment by spouting some stupid ass comment like, "Settle down, son, we're on vacation." Despite my best attempt to make lite of this pathetic scene, I couldn't ignore the look on his face, which was now permanently etched in my mind. Later, I discovered that Lukas had confided in a mutual friend that he would never go hunting with me again. For him, it was just too painful to watch. After this incident, I could now add "losing the respect of my son" to the alcohol damage report, and that one hit really, really hard.

Several months later, after some coaches and I had gone out to celebrate a baseball victory, I arrived home about 10:00pm. It was March 7, 2019. I greeted Deb, and everything seemed normal with our routine. After talking for a minute, she told me that she was going to walk the dog, so I went off to bed. As she left the house and got to the driveway, she noticed a light on in my truck and went to shut it off. As she fumbled around in the truck looking for the light source, she noticed a feed bucket in the back seat chock full of empty beer bottles. Early the next morning, as we were both getting ready for work, she confronted me about what she had found. I told her that some jackass had left the bottles down by the field, and I had forgotten to throw them away. Totally dejected, she just stared at me and said, "Do you really want to stick to that story?" I looked away because her eyes were so sad, and she appeared at a loss, as I had seen so many times before. I could now add lying to my wife to the damage report, and without getting myself in any deeper, I quickly finished my coffee and bolted off to work. On my drive in, Bucky's voice came over the radio, and I couldn't help but think about his journey to sobriety. He had done it, and in his very unique way, made others feel that they could do so as well. At this particular moment in time, his words had real meaning to me. As I drove on, the entirety of the situation hit me, and I began to assess it all. I had lied to Deb, my son didn't respect me anymore, and I was eighty pounds overweight and bloated beyond recognition. The lure of alcohol had done horrible damage to every aspect of my life, and as I took inventory of the carnage, I decided, once and for all, that I was done.

When I got home that evening, I apologized to Deb and came clean about how bad the drinking had accelerated in the past few years. I also told her that I would never lie to her or put her through any of this ever again. This time I was going to put the whole thing in the hands of the Good Lord. I found a group at my church who were facing the same problem. At first, I was concerned about going to the meetings because I thought I might be recognized, but I soon understood that the vanity of this sort of thinking was only going to hold me back.

After scaling over that small obstacle, I didn't give a shit who saw me or what anyone else thought. The people in this group were very special, and at one time in their lives, they had all been broken—some very badly. Hearing their testimonials made me realize that I wasn't alone, and it further demonstrated the raw damage that alcohol can inflict on everyone involved. The more of this I absorbed, the more I was able to see alcohol for what it was. As the days turned into months, my competitive spirit slowly returned, and my ability to fight became stronger and stronger. Reading the Bible became a much deeper and more meaningful experience, which helped immensely in strengthening my damaged spirit. Deb, courageously, was by my side yet again and showed me, as she always had, the true meaning of what it meant to love someone. Alcohol addiction is an unrelenting monster, and the unmotivated have no chance against it. I clearly proved that in 2014. But this time was different. All of this wonderful, powerful support was like having a fortress built around me, and it offered a chance against a scourge I had so willingly let through the front gates many years before.

As my journey progressed, my health gradually rebounded in ways I would have never imagined. I now slept through the night, and most importantly, the color of life returned to my eyes. Because I think clearer now, the thought of taking a drink repulses me, and more importantly, the deception of the lure of alcohol is completely understood. The hardest part of this journey was having to face the immense damage and the precious years wasted that resulted from my drinking. As bad as the damage was, the fact remains that I miraculously dodged many lethal bullets and would be remiss not to recognize the protection that God afforded me throughout my addiction. For instance, after I became sober, Deb shared with me what it was like for her to live through this ordeal. She told me about the night she found the cans in my truck and shared with me, for the first time, that she had actually been monitoring the inside of the vehicle for a while. She said that one day there would be a full case in the back seat, and the next time she checked, there would be nothing but empty beer cans. My deception was too much for her to deal with, and in a very somber moment, Deb revealed that she had made the decision to leave me on two separate occasions. Thankfully, God intervened both times and convinced her to stay. I could have (and should have) lost my wife during all of this, and if it weren't for her faith, that most certainly would have happened. I was given a second chance to make it right, and that opportunity, as well as where it came from, is so clearly understood now that I use it as my guide in everything I do.

I have been sober for three years and counting, made possible by some divine intervention, an incredible group of like-minded people, a selfless old man on the radio, and a loving wife and family who never gave up on me. I have also regained my competitive spirit and see drinking now as a formidable opponent in the arena, worthy of my respect but not worthy of my fear. They say alcoholism never goes away, and I believe that to be true, but based on the supporting cast that so blesses my life, and the fact that I now see alcohol for the scourge it is, I like my chances as this fight moves forward.

The world is full of people who needlessly suffer from this disease. Those who do are no different than anyone else except for the fact that they took a path that was full of deception and false promises. If you face an addiction of any kind, know that this problem is not unique to you and that there exist good and talented people who can help. Also, understand that no matter how far that you feel you have fallen down the hole, there is always a way to climb out. Life is precious, and it's worth the effort to get it back. You're not a loser or some outcast. You're a human being with dignity, and I promise that you can live again. Trust me, I was there, and I felt the seemingly inescapable grip addiction can have on a person's life. I know the horrors of thinking nobody understands what you're going through and the trauma of letting your loved ones down.

Getting through these dark times is absolutely possible, and the reward on the other end is greater than you could ever imagine. I say this because it's all about understanding that there is a way out, and if you can at least get to that point, anything can happen. I apologize if this comes across as preachy, as that's not my intent. I simply want to offer hope to everyone who finds themselves in a bad situation, coming from someone who has experienced the depths of despair and found his way out. It begins with believing in yourself again and letting that be the starting point for your recovery. I can assure you that the exhilaration of living again far exceeds any pain experienced on the road to getting there.

Three months into my journey towards sobriety, I received the awful news that Bill Buckner had died at his ranch in Idaho. He suffered from Lewy body dementia and, at the time of his death, was surrounded by family and friends. Bill and I will forever be linked to that fateful night at Shea, and he got hit harder than anyone because of it. The two of us took totally different paths in dealing with this ordeal, and I will forever admire the man for having the courage and strength to go on living his life the way he did and handling everything that was thrown at him the way that he had. Reflecting on how Bill faced adversity inspired me on my journey toward recovery, and he is one of the great examples of the resilient spirit that lives in us all. As I said before, Bill Buckner was one helluva ballplayer, but more importantly, he was one helluva man. I feel privileged to have known such a good and honorable soul.

· · ·

I am now fifty-nine years old, and for the first time in decades, I am completely sober. The journey to this point was the hardest and yet most rewarding thing I have ever done. I faced off against myself and found renewal and hope. The real treasure was regaining both my dignity and the respect of my family, for which there is no price. Through it all, Deb never left my side, and that, without question, gave me my life back. The greatest mistake I ever made was letting alcohol get between us, and the goal now is to live the years I have left with purpose. I still had one final hurdle to get over, but now I would do so with a clear and uncluttered mind. You see, much of life is about gaining wisdom, and I'm now wise enough to know that I first had to complete my journey to recovery before I could find the inner peace and the answers I had been searching for since 1986.

Chapter 15

THE MAN IN THE ARENA

... and who at worst, if he fails, at least he fails while daring greatly, so that his place shall never be with those cold and timid souls who neither know victory nor defeat.
—TEDDY ROOSEVELT

IN SO MANY WAYS, I was experiencing what it was like to live again, and one of the greatest attributes of being sober was getting back the clarity in my mind. It's not an exaggeration when they say that with sobriety, the colors of the world return and that everything is much sharper and better defined. All of this happened to me, and it has made living every day much deeper and so much more meaningful. Unfortunately, all of your problems don't just magically disappear when you give up alcohol, and there was a serious yet unresolved issue still affecting me that had nothing to do with drinking. Keep in mind, my journey down this dark path began because I was unable to reconcile some of the things that had happened to me years ago, and drinking or not, these remained unresolved.

It was on that trip I took with a friend to south Texas during hunting season (the one I described at the beginning of this book) when I revealed the nasty messages I had received after years of keeping them secret. I finally decided to tell someone because I was sober now, and my mind was clear and more rational. It was the right time, and he was the right person to share them with. I had just received the latest one of these emails a week earlier, and that's the one I gave him. As he read it over, he shook his head, completely dumbfounded, not by the email but by the fact I had kept it. Understanding the hurt I was attempting to laugh off, he chastised me in a very unrefined way and went on to describe, in vivid detail, the character of the guy who would send such a message. As you may remember, once he finished, and without saying another word, he pulled out his phone and read aloud Teddy Roosevelt's *The Man in the Arena,* which I had never heard before. Here's part of what he read:

> *It is not the critic who counts; not the man who points out how the strong man stumbles or where the doer of deeds could have done them better. The credit belongs to the man who is actually in the Arena, whose face is marred by dust and sweat and blood; who strives valiantly, who errs, who comes up short again and again; who spends himself in a worthy cause; who at best knows, in the end, the triumph of high achievement, and who at worst, if he fails, at least he fails while daring greatly so that his place shall never be with those cold and timid souls who neither know victory nor defeat.*

The first seven words immediately grabbed my attention, and because of that, I listened to every word like they were coming at me in slow motion. My heart pounded as he continued through the passage. It was all so obvious, and yet I had never heard anything like it. When he finished, I asked him to read it again. After he did, I asked him to read only the last two lines, and he obliged. I told him that I thought it was really good, but my mind was racing so fast I found it hard to concentrate.

I quickly moved our conversation to a different subject, but when we reached the hunting camp, and I was in my room alone, I pulled the speech up on my phone and read it for myself. In the stillness of the moment, I let the words flow through my mind. I knew, then and there, that I had found the answer which had escaped me for thirty-five years. I had finally identified the forces I could never understand. The passage had revealed them to me. They were the *cold and timid souls,* and now that I understood the nature of their being, they no longer had power over me. You see, you can't cure a disease until you properly identify it, and as I sat there alone in my room, I knew I had turned the corner once and for all. There are many diseases that are relatively easy to cure but left unchecked and unattended, they can wreak havoc on the human body.

The cold and timid souls are no different. Left unchecked, they can do immense damage, not to the body but to the spirit. These people offer nothing positive, peddling exclusively in ruin and shame. The solution to them is simple, understand that they come from a gutless position, fueled by ignorance and contempt, then move on. Who are these people?

They're the jackasses who sit in the stands and hurl personal insults at the combatants in the Arena. They're the tough guys who mock and taunt you as you walk off the field in defeat. They're the self-appointed experts who claim to understand what's inside of your head. The ones who completely disregard any concept of the winning spirit that fills the hearts of those who dare to compete—while never having competed themselves. They're schoolyard bullies who prey solely on the defenseless because they themselves are too cowardly to take on a real challenge. And yes, they are Internet warriors who sit behind their keyboards typing nasty emails to those who fought in the Arena and failed.

The very nature of what they do is as pathetic as the jackals mocking the lions after the deer got away. My greatest revelation from the Roosevelt quote was that they could call me loser, choker, or whatever they wanted, but that which defines them (cold and timid souls) is the lowest and saddest identifier of all. For thirty-four years, I had allowed these people to dictate my moods and set the narrative of my life. I provided them a platform and was blinded to their insignificance due to their ferocity and timing. The cold and timid souls prey on fallen combatants like buzzards, who could never catch a meal of their own, and yet I had made the unfathomable error of dignifying their existence by allowing them in. They have no idea what the inside of an Arena even looks like but have the audacity to mock those of us who do. If I could have somehow stayed patient during the tsunami that engulfed me and not turned to alcohol, I would have realized this long ago, but the fact is, I made a stupid ass decision that allowed these sideline dwellers inside my head. And I paid for that, heavily.

I loved everything about Roosevelt's timeless speech, especially the opening line, "It's not the critic who counts." He's not saying that all criticism deserves ignoring. It's much more specific than that. For instance, a food critic goes to a restaurant and doesn't like the food and says so. That's not what he is going after. Or perhaps the sportswriter who writes about a quarterback having a terrible game after throwing four interceptions. That's not it either. Roosevelt was talking about the critic who takes it to a personal level and opines about the spirit or the grit of an athlete, or worse, suggests that he knows what was in the mind of the person in the Arena. You know, things like "He was intimidated," "He should put a dress on," "He didn't want it bad enough," "He just didn't care," "The stage was too big for him," "He's nothing but a loser," or my favorite, "That team just wanted it more." These are the critics that don't count because it's impossible for them to know what the hell is in the mind of those who are out there, and yet, they have no qualms about portraying themselves to their audience as if they do. Oddly, this simultaneously personifies both ignorance and arrogance. These critics will always exist, and although you can't realistically fight back, you can ignore them, accept them as the cold and timid souls they are, and move on.

The closing line from Roosevelt's speech "... who neither know victory nor defeat" resonated with me as well. These six words express, in very clear terms, the essential role losing can play in the world of a competitor. Much can be learned from being on the losing end of a battle because the pain is so great, it forges you into something stronger. Losing is actually a wonderful opportunity for growth if you allow it to be, and therefore, should never bring you shame. The fact that the cold and timid souls mock those who lose demonstrates perfectly that they understand nothing about the riches the Arena can offer. In other words, they mock what they don't understand, and by doing so, mock themselves in the eyes of true competitors.

Although you might find it strange that I never heard the words of Teddy Roosevelt before I did, it happened exactly how I described it. The sad fact was that I never sought anything that could have helped me escape the storm that had engulfed my life. Alcohol played a key role in choosing the road that I did, but because of the way I was raised, openly seeking help or answers to the underlying issues was never part of the equation. That was a costly mistake. Fortunately, my introduction to the quote coincided perfectly with my sobriety and the two of them, together, helped me make sense of it all.

• • •

Sometimes in life, something very simple can trigger understanding. This quote did just that, and it brought clarity at a time when I needed it most. The cold and timid souls are very real, as are some of the critics who swim with them in the very same waters. To understand them the way I do now has afforded me a clarity to see things in a much more profound way. You see, the prudent thing is to just ignore them and move on. I not only get that, I lived it. However, when their actions become so egregious that they begin to mock your competitive soul, that's when you have to fight back. Otherwise, you risk losing the very spirit that put you in the Arena in the first place.

Chapter 16

A SACRED CODE BROKEN

Be aware of those who don't fight back. Sooner or later they will.
—J. RACHELLE

IN REALITY, competitors are usually the furthest thing from a cold and timid soul. In fact, you'll rarely see those in the Arena partake in the mocking or shaming of their fellow combatants—especially after the contest is settled. The reason for this is that competitors understand what it's like to be in the Arena, as well as the effort and sacrifice required to be there. There is a certain and undeniable respect afforded between those who dare to do something special and have the spirit to give winning their best shot. For example, Mookie Wilson never uttered a negative word about Bill Buckner. In fact, he did just the opposite. Dave Henderson never mocked Donnie Moore, doing just the opposite as well. It comes down to the respect they had for both the battle and the spirit of their opponent. It's also called class, and for the most part, those in the Arena understand and abide by the concept. Unfortunately, this is not always the case, as on rare occasions, this respect or sacred code is violated.

For the past three decades, I made it a point to avoid books written about the '86 series because the subject had devolved into something resembling the Wild West. I saw no productive reason to enter those waters and have read very little on the topic. However, in 2020, a friend brought to my attention that Ron Darling had trashed my athletic character in his most recent book.* I told him that I didn't believe it, as Ron had no reason to do anything of the kind. Sadly, I was shown the copy, and sure enough, Ron Darling had made the decision to go down that road and align himself with the cold and timid souls who had been after me for years. What's worse, he wrote it decades after the series was played. In the past something like this would have sent me straight to the convenience store on a beer run, but not anymore. The truth is, I was tired of putting up with it. Tired of playing by a set of rules that tells me to sit back and accept any insult thrown my way. Yes, I lost Game 6 after being one pitch away from winning it and have always accepted responsibility for that. But I'm not accepting the shit Ron Darling published in his book. My response here is not about tit for tat or getting back at Darling. I don't give a rat's ass about either one. This is about right and wrong. It's about showing a clear example of some of the degrading and reckless things that were thrown my way. By me doing so, perhaps you'll gain a better insight of what comes out of the no-holds-barred world of bashing players on the losing end of big games. Please note, I'm not fighting back against a drunken fan who hurled every imaginable insult at me. That guy should be ignored. Ron Darling, on the other hand, won't be.

For starters, Darling's hit-piece came out of nowhere and thirty-three years after the fact. In all sincerity, who does that kind of shit? His attack was shallow, gutless, and had only one purpose—score cheap points with his readers by demeaning someone he thought was too beaten and weak to swing back. There was no regard to decency, no regard to shame, and certainly no regard to what stood on the other side of the belittlement. The humiliation

---

* *108 Stitches* by Ron Darling with Daniel Paisner, pages 128–129. Copyright 2019, St. Martins Press.

and embarrassment his words would potentially bring upon me or my family were never considered.

I knew Ron from the time I played with the Mets, and he was one of the guys I congratulated when I went to their locker room after Game 7. Darling was a damn good pitcher then, as he was throughout most of his career, and I had no issues with him during the short time we knew each other. For some reason, in 2019, he decided to write a "tell-all" book where he made a number of disparaging comments about former Mets teammates. Far worse, he shared a locker room story about beloved Met's announcer Bob Murphy which appeared way out of bounds and some might argue, humiliating to Bob. There was a certain coldness to all of it. Despite the fact that nothing appeared to be off-limits, perhaps the oddest thing was that Ron seems to want to portray himself as some sort of great "team player," only to then turn around and trash some of the very guys who fought alongside him in the trenches. As it turned out, one of his "revelations" led to a defamation lawsuit with which he was served following publication. In another section of his book, and for reasons I still don't understand, Darling decided to mock and demean me. Even worse, he centered his attack on a game I played with the Mets in 1985 and at a time when I was injured.

Anyone who has ever played in the big leagues understands how difficult it is to make the adjustment from the minors to the majors, especially from the mound, and in this particular game, nothing I did worked. Simply put, I got my ass shelled like I never had in my life. It was an early June game in 1985 against Philadelphia when I came in for the Mets as a middle reliever. Two pitchers that day gave up ten runs each, and I was one of them. The Phillies went on to score an unheard of 26 total runs. As a young pitcher, and after a beat down like that, you have no choice but to lick your wounds and move on with your career, which is exactly what I did, with the numbers to back it up. Ron Darling, however, decided he wanted to highlight this performance and use it in an effort to belittle me as an athlete. He wrote mockingly about my time on the mound that day but never mentioned that I was battling a significant injury on my plant foot, a splintered bone in my toe. Choosing to omit that detail was one of the many ways Darling kept his audience from seeing the whole picture as he laid the foundation for the narrative he was creating leading up to Game 6. He said that there was a "give up" in me and that I wanted to be anywhere but on the mound. He had the arrogance to speak for all of the Mets players by suggesting that they all saw me as a losing player. Ron used a one inning sample out of the massive number of games I had played in my life, and that was enough for him to publicize to the world that I was a loser. This, on its face, was both reckless and deceptive. It was also stupid. Despite the fact that I was only twenty-three years old at the time, I was the furthest thing from the losing player he was trying to portray. I had won at every conceivable level I ever played, starting with the Babe Ruth state championship when I was fifteen. I won in high school, college, in the minor leagues, in the major leagues, in the playoffs, and in the World Series. The résumé I had built going into the Game 6 was both accomplished and extremely rare. But none of that mattered to Darling, who portrayed me as a loser going into Game 6 and gave the impression to his readers that everyone knew it. This act of deception broke every code of decency usually understood by professional athletes, and yet it went completely unchecked. Far worse, he continually hid critical details from his readers. The most glaring omission was the fact that I, the "losing player" he courageously mocked from behind his keyboard, had saved Game 1 of the 1986 World Series, which ironically was the very same game Ron Darling lost. Didn't his readers deserve to know this minor detail?

Anyway, Darling continued the mockery by suggesting that the whole Mets team was "giddy" with excitement during Game 6 when I walked out to the mound. Let's pause here for a moment because I have two serious issues with that. The first is a grown man using the word "giddy" while mocking a fellow competitor. The second issue, especially when considering the outcome of Game 1, is what exactly was he so "giddy" about? None of it makes any sense. He then took it to the level of contempt by writing, "It felt to us like

McNamara (Mac) was waving the white flag and giving up on the game."* This particular remark referred to my entry into Game 6. He actually printed that shit in his book. He painted a picture for his readers that portrayed him and his Mets teammates celebrating in the dugout as Mac threw in the towel by putting me in the game. I'm baffled by his willingness to be so disrespectful, and I find his deceit and attempt at mockery bizarre. Here's why. Going into Game 6, I was the established closer for the American League Champion Red Sox, with an ERA of 1.41. In the postseason, I had closed my last three outings, including Game 1 of the World Series, and had only given up one run in those three appearances. Just how in the hell is McNamara waving white flags and giving up on the game by putting me in? When the established closer enters an epic World Series game at a critical time, that moment and the intensity surrounding it should be remembered for what it represented to the game of baseball, and yet Darling was hell-bent to disparage it. Why? Again, it made no sense, but it's a good example of the willfully misleading shit that Darling, and people like him, got away with. Ron, who portrays himself as an authentic and fair-minded guy, chose to omit these critical details for one simple reason—they didn't equate to the "losing player" narrative he was desperately trying to develop. He took one of the greatest and most intense games in the history of our sport and selfishly reduced it in an attempt to demean me. You expect this garbage from the cold and timid souls, but not Darling, a former player who now analyzes baseball games for a living.

The most frustrating part about all of this? I was being mocked by someone who wasn't even there. During the most crucial part of the epic Game 6, Ron Darling wasn't even in the stadium. As hard as this is to fathom, it's absolutely true. Darling was in street clothes, driving down the freeway and away from Shea while his Mets teammates were on the cusp of losing the World Series. This fact is so stunning that it's hard to even grasp. Think about the balls it takes to

* *108 Stitches* by Ron Darling with Daniel Paisner, page 128. Copyright 2019, St. Martins Press.

mock an opposing pitcher who was actually in the throes of a battle while you, at the same time, abandoned your team and left the ballpark. You see, Darling wasn't there for the ninth inning. But I was, and I was in the Arena, in uniform and battling my ass off. He never saw the situation I faced with a runner on second, no outs, and Game 6 of the World Series hanging in the balance on every pitch. As he trashed me in his book, he mentions none of this, nor does he mention the fact that we fought ourselves out of that nasty situation, holding the Mets scoreless and sending the game into extra innings. Again, the whole thing was disconcerting. The guy who was in the Arena fighting was mocked by the guy who had abandoned his team. That not only shocks the senses, it defiles the game of baseball.

There was an even greater irony unfolding here. Around the time Darling made the decision to turn his car around and return to the stadium, I was still in there battling, in the tenth inning and just one pitch away from winning the World Series. Despite this well-known fact, Darling still chose to write in his book, thirty-three years later, about the "waving of white flags" and "being giddy."

I was one pitch away.

This was not only disgraceful, but it also insulted the intelligence of anyone who knew the real story. But it got worse. Darling actually printed in his book that I was the one who threw the wild pitch and that I gave up the game-winning ground ball that got through Bill Buckner's legs, despite the fact that I wasn't even in the game when those things occurred. This book mind you was circulated throughout the country, and yet not a single "baseball expert" called him out on this blatant error. Seriously, wouldn't you think that before going to press with a nasty "tell-all" book that a baseball analyst like Darling would have time for a quick Google search? After all, this was one of the most famous moments in baseball history, and since he wasn't in the dugout to see it for himself, maybe a little research could have helped him get the facts right. The point of all of this is, despite his shameless attempt to mock me, Darling had the audacity to give his readers the impression that he was with his team watching it all go down. This gave phony credibility to his grossly inaccurate story. It also clearly demonstrates that rules and standards are not necessary when trashing a "losing player."

By the time the game ended, Darling had actually made it back to the stadium in time to celebrate the Game 6 victory with his teammates … in his street clothes. While he celebrated, I was in our locker room, mentally and physically battered, facing every reporter after the most grueling defeat a player could ever experience. The irony of this whole scene might escape others, but it doesn't escape me.

You'll have to forgive me for taking this liberty, but at some point in life, you have to set the record straight, defend your name, and stand up to a guy like Ron Darling. There's an unwritten rule in professional sports that seems to discourage athletes from defending themselves, but when does enough become enough? That time came when he chose to demean me as a competitor in order to score cheap points with his readers.

They say to take the high road in situations like this, but if taking the high road means guys like Darling get to set the narrative on something as important to me as my competitive spirit, then I take exception to what "taking the high road" even means. In other words, what they are saying is to have no pride and stay silent as someone methodically and falsely picks you apart. I can tell you firsthand that staying silent only emboldens guys like Ron and that nobody should ever allow themselves to be publicly and deceitfully shamed by guys like him. Maybe if more people called out bullshit like this, there would be less of it polluting the world of sports. One can only hope.

I highlighted this so you could see a great example of what the Wild West was capable of producing. Darling, and people like him, took that epic loss, then, at their own discretion, attached anything they wanted to it and did so with impunity. There were few rules, standards, objectivity, or perspective. After all, they were just trashing a "losing player," so what did it matter if they didn't get all the facts right or took a few liberties along the way? I am far from unique when it comes to the shaming of athletes who have lost big games, and to be perfectly honest, the whole thing troubles me. A person's spirit is sacred and to have it mocked by those who haven't the slightest clue is an assault on the soul. It's not just the attack that is troubling, but rather the sheer number of people who are willing to do it as the rest sit quietly and accept it as normal behavior.

In the end, despite what Ron or others chose to say about me, one thing is irrefutable; I stayed in there and fought, and when I wasn't on the mound, I never left my Red Sox teammates, and I sure as hell never left that stadium. Try to imagine being portrayed as a quitter and a loser by a guy like Darling. Only then will you sample a small taste of what my world was like after missing that pitch in 1986.

Whether it was an anonymous email, some jackass in the stands, or a guy scoring cheap points with his readers, all of these things were part and parcel of my life. Rather than defending myself, I chose alcohol and became their victim, ushering in shame and confusion. Throughout my life, I prided myself for possessing great inner strength and mental toughness, but when it came time to use those gifts to protect myself, I failed miserably.

• • •

A lot can be learned from the journey I've been on, and my hope is that you can see these things as clearly as I do now. When daring to do great things, there will always be those who will do their best to break your spirit. The sooner you learn this truth, the easier it will be to navigate as you venture in and out of your chosen Arena. It takes a special kind of mindset to go for things in this world, and I admire those who strive for excellence. I always have.

The Arena is not for the meek, which is why they will never benefit from what it offers. Don't make the mistakes I did and let the cold and timid souls impact who you are. Be better than that. Understand them for who they are and keep competing for whatever it is you seek. It will be the greatest and most rewarding thing you can do because in the end, you put yourself out there, and that, in and of itself, will separate you from the masses.

Chapter 17

LETTING GO

You don't need strength to let go of something. What you really need is understanding. —GUY FINLEY

ON A PERFECT SPRING EVENING not long ago, all was quiet and still on our usually active campus. I drove a golf cart down to the baseball field to watch the sunset, one of my favorite things to do. My mind had cleared from the haze brought on by years of drinking, and the colors in my world were brighter and the air crisper to my senses. At the age of fifty-nine, I sat there alone, surrounded by sounds that only nature could provide. The view before me was one to behold, and as I took it all in, memories began to flow freely like never before.

I reminisced about my life's journey, and the images played out so vividly in my mind that it was like watching a movie. I was giving myself permission to relive some of my earlier achievements, which in the past, I had strictly forbidden. Memories of Westlake and winning the state championship all came back, followed by my time at Texas, the National Championship, and being named MVP in Omaha. I thought to myself, "Son-of-a-bitch, at one point, you were considered the best collegiate pitcher in America." My thoughts turned to the retirement of my Westlake jersey and my induction into The University of Texas Hall of Honor. I reflected on turning pro, my journey through the gauntlet, pitching for the Single-A championship team, getting to start in the Double-A All-Star Game, and being named Reliever of the Year in Triple-A. I thought about getting the save against the California Angels in Game 5 of the ALCS, which is still considered one of the greatest playoff games in major league history. I remembered being on the mound and striking out the side to end Game 7 of the 1986 ALCS, sending Boston and their incredible fans to the World Series. Then, for the very first time, I gave myself a chance to appreciate the fact that I had actually pitched in the World Series and walked out of Shea Stadium with a save. I had never given that achievement its proper place, but at this moment, I understood just how special and rare it was.

My focus returned to the baseball field before me, and my mind took me to the moment when my teams celebrated unrestrained after winning back-to-back state championships. I then remembered the wonderful times I had as a coach and all of the players I so dearly loved. The tranquility of this moment and the memories that it helped bring to the surface had lifted my spirits, bringing a smile to my face and pride to my heart.

Then, out of nowhere, as if I wasn't allowed to enjoy these forbidden memories any longer, a voice inside of me said, "Wait a minute, not so fast. Let's not forget that it was you who cost one of the greatest college teams in history a chance at the National Championship." Yes, that was true. "And let's not forget," the voice continued, "that with bases loaded, you hit a batter in Game 4 of the ALCS, costing your team that critical game." True again. "If that's not enough, remember it was also you who had a 0–2 count and was one strike away from winning a World Championship, didn't get it done, and then followed that by getting hammered in Game 7. Do I need to remind you that you have the dubious distinction of losing Games 6 and 7 of the World Series?" Unfortunately, it was all true, and no surprise that these thoughts appeared because they always had. They were an ever-present part of my life for the past thirty-five years. This time, however, something very different happened. The smile that came from reflecting on the positive memories never left my face, nor did my incredible sense of pride. Even better, there was no sinking feeling in the pit of my stomach after I kindly reminded myself of past failures. This was the moment when it happened, the moment I realized for the first time the true meaning of the events that had so changed my life.

I had finally granted myself permission to see these things for what they were, and it gave me an overwhelming sense of peace. What I had experienced on my journey was a series of rare opportunities to accomplish great things. Very few are ever allowed this chance. I realized that fixating on failures while never smelling the roses of success was one of my most costly mistakes. What really mattered was striving for excellence and giving everything I had to make the most of the chances I was given. I was the *Man in the Arena,* and although winning was always my only objective, that's not what the Arena is about. The Arena is about the will in a man's heart and the skills that he has so painstakingly refined to give himself the best chance at winning. It's about passion, desire, and having the courage to put it all on the line, being fully aware that pain and humiliation are lurking around every corner. That's the true meaning of the Arena, and in the end, all that matters.

Coming to this realization and knowing I always gave everything I had, provided an undeniable sense of both pride and relief. Most importantly, I felt whole again. I now realized that the Arena had been a true blessing and not the devil's den I had later made it out to be. A person is defined by the depths of their soul and the passion in which they live, and the Arena is where these qualities are forged and put on full display. This is why it is so important—not because it defines winners and losers, but because it defines the human spirit inside us all. Teddy Roosevelt masterfully explained it over one hundred years ago, and I regret having never read his words before, as well as all of the time wasted before I did.

As I sat there motionless, with a new appreciation for the journey I'd been on, I vowed to begin living again. There would be no more looking back and wasting valuable time on things I could not change or toxic people I could never please. No more alcohol or other bullshit that would distance me from my wife and family. I had finally broken free, giving myself permission to let it go, and there was nothing like it in the world.

Escaping from the darkness is a feeling so powerful that only those who have been there can adequately describe. It changes every aspect of how you see the world. You see, if doing your best and falling short brings you shame, then there's something fundamentally wrong with the way you're approaching things. I was one hundred percent responsible for allowing myself to go to that dark place, and that will remain the greatest regret of my life. With that said, there's nothing about this journey I would ever consider changing. The Arena gave me the only life I have ever known and allowed me to experience living from every dimension. The wisdom I gained from entering its gates has enlightened me in ways that otherwise would have never been possible. I get that now.

As the sun inched closer to the horizon, my mind took me to one last, very difficult place. It was a question actually, a somewhat haunting question, one that had been asked of me many times over the years—*don't you wish you would have made that pitch in 1986?* The reflections of this evening had given me a new perspective to see things in ways I never had before, and the answer to that question was suddenly much clearer than it had ever been. Although I did everything in my power and had every confidence I would strike out Ray Knight, it just didn't happen, and that can never be changed.

What did happen, however, was that the events of that October evening set me on a path that tested every fiber of my being, and from that, I have experienced life in ways few others ever will. Had I made that pitch, I would have never seen my high school teams dogpiling on the mound. I would have never experienced the depths of love and dedication shown to me by Deb and my children. I would have never known what it was like to enter the Arena against myself, leading to an unbridled appreciation for life. What's more, I would have never had the faith that I do now, and for me, that's the greatest gift of all. Making that pitch would have almost certainly changed my life in ways that are far removed from where I am today, so the answer to that question is no, and rest assured, I can live with that now.

As I looked over the baseball field, the most relaxing breeze came out of nowhere, carrying with it a sense of peace I hadn't felt in years. The sun had just gone down, leaving behind a breathtaking orange sky. With a smile on my face and tears in my eyes, I felt my father's voice.

"You did a good job out there, Calvin; I'm really proud of you."

My high school coach, Howard Bushong. It's hard to describe what this man means to me.

My South Texas hunting buddies, Dave, Darren, Max and Ryan.

LUKAS, RHETT, AND KYLE MARTIN

I was blessed to coach so many incredible young men in my life and these three were no exception. All got drafted and Kyle made it all the way.

Players and parents from the past surprised me with a party. I spoke in the book about what a treasure these guys were. To see their successes as adults couldn't make me prouder.

DEBBIE SCHIRALDI

She never left my side and that gave me my life back. The best day of my life is when she walked through the door when I was living in Jackson, Mississippi. She's an amazing mother, a kind and gentle soul, and the love of my life.

INDEX